Endorseme

"What I love most about Chandra is her genuine love for people. Couple that with the passion she has for this generation of girls to know they are cherished by the almighty God, and you have a winning combination! I know thousands will be empowered by this book."
—**Natalie Grant**, four-time female vocalist of the year (GMA Dove Awards)

"Chandra makes it simple. Insecure? Family falling apart? Bruised relationships? Chandra takes the reader by the hand, walks her through her complicated life, and gives her simple solutions using the Word of God. She makes the Bible applicable, understandable, and personal to each girl who picks up this book."
—**Jenna Lucado**, author of *Redefining Beautiful: What God Sees When God Sees You* with **Max Lucado**

"This is exactly what young people need. Soaked in scriptural truth, sprinkled with grace, and saturated with the countercultural messages God wants them to hear, *Cherished* is a book that I'm excited to give to young people searching for hope."
—**Daniel Darling**, author of *Teen People of the Bible*

"You can hear Chandra's heartbeat for young women to know and love God as you read through the pages of *Cherished*."
—**Sarah Bragg**, author of *Body. Beauty. Boys.*

Cherished

Discovering the freedom to love and be loved

By Chandra Peele

NEW HOPE
PUBLISHERS
Birmingham, Alabama

New Hope® Publishers
P. O. Box 12065
Birmingham, AL 35202-2065
www.newhopepublishers.com

New Hope Publishers is a division of WMU®.

Library of Congress Cataloging-in-Publication Data

Peele, Chandra.
  Cherished : discovering the freedom to love and be loved / by Chandra Peele.
    p. cm.
  Includes bibliographical references and index.
  ISBN-13: 978-1-59669-250-3 (sc : alk. paper)
  ISBN-10: 1-59669-250-2 (sc : alk. paper) 1. Love--Religious aspects--Christianity--Textbooks. 2. God--Love--Textbooks. I. Title.
  BV4639.P34 2009
  241'.4--dc22
                        2009006866

ISBN-10: 1-59669-250-2
ISBN-13: 978-1-59669-250-3

N094145 • 0809 • 3.5M1

dedication

To Bruce, my loving husband and best friend,
I love you!

And to

my daughters, Lindsey and Holly,
the two girls I cherish the most.

I love you!

And to

the ones reading this;
your heavenly Father did more than dedicate a book to you,
He gave His one and only Son
all because He loves YOU!

You are *cherished* by God!

Table of Contents

Hearts at War

Sitting at my departure gate, preparing for my flight and thinking back on the weekend, my heart was troubled. The girls' conference had been great and the worship was wonderful! But I couldn't shake the painful stories I heard at the end of my last session. More girls than ever before waited in line to speak with me. Most of these girls were believers in Jesus Christ and they needed someone to hear their story, someone to give them hope in their seemingly hopeless situation. They desperately needed someone to "fix" it. Someone to love them in the middle of the good, the bad, and the ugly.

- *What's wrong with me? Why is my life so empty?*
- *Why do I feel so unloved?*
- *Why don't I have friends?*
- *Why is my family so miserable?*
- *Why don't I have a boyfriend?*
- *I feel so ugly.*
- *I'm so lonely.*

Over and over I heard their desperate cries. Although each story was different they can all be described with one word...*hopeless*. These girls were Christians yet they were living in bondage. Why weren't they experiencing the freedom found in Christ?

Once on the plane, leaning my head back as the force of the jets pressed me against the seat, I felt as though I was on my way to a meeting with God. Looking in awe at the beauty of the puffy white clouds against the blue sky, I began to talk to my heavenly Father. The sun's rays pierced through the clouds like open arms. I cried out to Him: "Father, why are so many of your daughters hurting? I know You love them. Everywhere You send me, people are hurting. Lord, give me the words to say; words that offer hope."

With my Bible in the bag in front of me, I felt an urge to read His Word. As I flipped the pages, they fell open and Matthew 22 caught my eye. Jesus said:

"'You must love the LORD your God with all your heart, all your soul, and all your mind.' This is the first and greatest commandment. A second is equally important: 'Love your neighbor as yourself.' The entire law and all the demands of the prophets are based on these two commandments."
—Matthew 22:37–40

Out of my desperate cry I believe the Lord God spoke to me through His Word instantly. God listens *and* He speaks! I have read and heard sermons on these verses many times in my life but I saw something new this time.

Number one, I see we *must* love the Lord first. What I noticed second is the new thing He taught me. Love your neighbor *as* yourself.

I got it! If we love God with all we are, then *He* will be our focus. Not *me.* And if He is our focus, then our confidence in Him will allow us to be confident in ourselves. We will get our self-worth from Him and not from the world. When we trust in His love for us, then we will have the freedom to be who He created us to be. And then we will have the desire to love others.

Many girls experience "religion," but many have never experienced spiritual freedom. Discovering what it means to be free in Christ changed my life! Every day I come to a better understanding of what it means to

I got it! If we love God with all we are, then He will be our focus. Not me. And if He is our focus, then our confidence in Him will allow us to be confident in ourselves. We will get our self-worth from Him and not from the world.

Cherished

live and walk in freedom. My prayer as I write this study is that while God teaches me, abundant freedom and love will spill over to you.

Here is a little taste…a little bite to nibble on to get you started.

For you have been called to live in freedom, my brothers and sisters. But don't use your freedom to satisfy your sinful nature. Instead, use your freedom to serve one another in love. *For the whole law can be summed up in this one command: "Love your neighbor as yourself." But if you are always biting and devouring one another, watch out! Beware of destroying one another.*
—Galatians 5:13–15 (author's emphasis)

Can you see how freedom and love have a lot to do with each other? Read it again.

Pray that the Father will prepare *your eyes* and *your ears,* so *your heart* can be reshaped to look more like His. I am convinced and persuaded that God made you to love. If God is love and He lives in us, by the Holy Spirit, then I have to ask this question: Why is it so hard for us to love?

Not chicken fingers, clothes, popularity, applause; those things are easy to love. We have developed our very own definition of what *love* means. We can apply it to almost everything! How crazy is it to think this same word can be used to describe our feelings for a new puppy or food or a certain brand of handbag and also for people?

It's time to prepare for battle, time for some basic training. It's time to go back and study God's Word. It's time to learn how to *love* God, how to *love* other people, and how to *love* a new humble and grateful "self." Yes. You read it right. You need to learn how to love you—the one God created to love Him and to love others with a genuine, stripped-down-to-nothing, heartfelt, kind, caring, holy LOVE. By applying Matthew 22:37–40 to your life you'll find freedom and discover a new kind of love—God's perfect love! By the way…in case you didn't know, He's the One who first loved you.

Now, get your Bible and a pen. *Cherished* has been written to get you into God's Word, to challenge you to memorize Scripture. If you don't

It's time to prepare for battle, time for some basic training. It's time to go back and study God's Word.

know where one of the books in the Bible is located, simply go to the front of your Bible—to the contents page—and there it will show you where to turn. By doing this you will quickly become familiar with your Bible, and it will become more special to you.

My Prayer

Lord, I'm ready to begin. Prepare my heart and my mind as I study Your Word. My desire is to understand these teachings so that I can apply them to my life every day. Lord, be my guide and help me keep my commitment to spend this time with You. It is my desire to know You more. Amen.

Choose Jesus
Choose Freedom
Choose Love

The Spirit of the Sovereign LORD is upon me, because the LORD has appointed me to bring good news to the poor. He has sent me to comfort the brokenhearted and to announce that captives will be released and prisoners will be freed
—Isaiah 61:1

To live freely means you are not held or bound by anything physically or mentally.

Before you begin this session take a moment to stop and pray. Ask God to open your eyes and heart to hear His Truth as you study His Word. Are you ready to learn something new? You'll need your Bible and a pen. Got it? Then let's begin.

Freedom. Maybe you've never given this seven-letter word much thought, so let's quickly review its meaning. To live freely means you are not held or bound by anything physically or mentally. Freedom encompasses several synonyms or related words that are noteworthy for every young lady: self-determination; liberty; choice; free will. God desires us to be free, and freedom and love have a lot more in common than you might think. After all God is love, and true freedom is found in Him. My hope is that after studying God's Word in this session you will experience both freedom and love in your life more than ever before.

There are many verses in the Bible that teach about freedom. Chapter 5 of the Book of Galatians is one of my favorites, and it's also a great place for us to begin. Paul, the author, was sent by God to help clear up some confusion among new believers in the region of Galatia. They were struggling between the gospel (freedom given by grace to those who have faith in Jesus Christ) and legalism (man-made rules and conditions set up by people who misunderstood the Jewish law). Since Jewish law and tradition had been all the people knew for generations, they were confused. And some people were pressuring the Galatians to go back to the law. But Paul had good news for Christians! Those who have faith in Jesus Christ have been set free from the old bondages.

Open your Bible and read chapter 5 of the Book of Galatians.

Now look back at verse 1. I love it! Christians are no longer under the old law. We don't have to live by ritual or custom. Jesus Christ came to set us free!

Look down at chapter 5, verse 6 now. In Christ Jesus, circumcision (a traditional religious act) doesn't matter. The only thing that counts is faith expressing itself through love. In other words, no good deed is good enough. Only faith in Jesus Christ will set you free. Romans 4:5 says: *"But people are counted as righteous, not because of their work, but because of their faith in God who forgives sinners."*

> Faith believes in things unseen. Grace is a gift from God, and so is the faith it takes to believe. Graciously accept this gift and be thankful to God, the One who gives the gift. Look at your pinky finger. It is little and weak, just like you without faith. But with faith, you are mighty and strong because of the power of God through Jesus.
> —From *Priceless*, by Chandra Peele

Do you know what *self-righteous* means? Chandra's definition: It's when a person thinks she is good enough, spiritual enough, smart enough, or wealthy enough to enter the kingdom of God. But the reality is that salvation comes only through faith in Jesus Christ. Just remember self-righteousness is self-right, and it breeds pride.

Cherished

For it is by grace you have been saved, through faith—and this not from yourselves, it is the gift from God—not by works, so that no one can boast.
—Ephesians 2:8–9 (NIV)

Paul is a great teacher. He doesn't assume we already know everything he is teaching, so he explains himself so we can better apply these teachings to our own life. In Galatians 5, verse 16, <u>Paul tells us how we should live, in the Spirit. Then he warns us by telling us exactly what falls under the sinful nature.</u>

When you see the sinful nature spelled out in these verses, there are some real ugly actions on the list, wouldn't you agree? Some of these may be a little too familiar. Or just the opposite; you may be saying "I would never…" Be careful! Stay alert! The thief's (the devil's) purpose is to steal and kill and destroy (John 10:10*a*). And these are just a few tricks in his bag. Remember that sin is *anything* you do that is not pleasing to God. Don't be so quick to say *never* and don't be so quick to judge others.

Read Galatians 5:19–21 again.

Paul gives a list of actions and desires that keep you from experiencing spiritual freedom. In fact, they cast you into bondage. So keep away from these sins. If you are tempted by any of these be aware of that, then turn around and run away as fast as you can! List the sins found in verses 19–21.

> Sexual immorality, impurity, debauchery, idolatry, witchcraft, hatred, discord, jealousy, fits of rage, selfish ambition, dissentions, factions, envy, drunkenness, orgies

Remember you are called to live in freedom! The key is to stay as far away from sin as you can. This means making good choices. Are there any specific areas where you are getting too close to sin? Perhaps your choices reflect the world's ideals rather than godliness. Choose to live by the Spirit within you.

Read Matthew 16:23–28.

Spend a few moments thinking about these verses. Pray that God will give you a better understanding of His Word. What is the Holy Spirit speaking to you through this message? How are you following Jesus? Write your thoughts.

Read Galatians 5:22–23 again.

The fruit of the Spirit consists of love, joy, peace, patience, kindness, goodness, faithfulness, gentleness, and self-control. These are character traits and virtues of Jesus Christ Himself. They are produced only in the hearts of those who choose to live for Him and are given by the Holy Spirit. Notice the first trait mentioned is love.

It's really cool when you think about it. It's supernatural—something that only comes when we spend more time with Jesus. Think about it this way: When you hang out with the same people all the time you pick up their habits and mannerisms, good or bad. The same can be said when you have a relationship with Jesus Christ; however, everything he has modeled is good!

Freedom in Christ Is...

Write down and memorize the fruit of the Spirit. Use them as a spirit check to keep you reflecting Him. Get nine sticky notes or pieces of paper and write one of the virtues on each one. For example, write *love* on one and *joy* on another, and so on. Then stick them around the edge of your mirror. Every day, do a self-check and ask the Lord to show you if you are lacking in one or more of these qualities. If one particular virtue comes to mind that you really need to work on, place that paper in the middle of the mirror to remind you of it. Pray and spend some time in the Word. Once God has changed your heart and you've filled up with His Word, you can move the paper back to the edge of the mirror. Remember, the fruit of the Spirit is a gift, so when you get one trait, you get all nine. As a result, you are free to love God and free to serve and love your neighbor.

It's also important to note that selfishness is not represented at all in the nine. Once selfishness appears it kills the fruit like worms attacking apples on a tree. So when you have a bad attitude, it's obvious that you aren't producing fruit. Selfishness keeps you from producing any fruit at all.

If you were to take a spirit test now what would you find growing?

Philippians 4:8 is another great verse for doing a spirit check. *"Fix your thoughts on what is true, and honorable, and right, and pure, and lovely, and admirable. Think about things that are excellent and worthy of praise."*

Does this sound like your thought life? Memorize this verse too.

Are you enjoying this study of God's Word? Do you understand that as a Christian you have been set free in Christ? Only through freedom in Christ can you experience liberty in your life. Freedom…what a priceless gift to all who believe in Jesus Christ!

♥ Freedom in Jesus is when you have peace no matter what your circumstance.
♥ Freedom in Jesus is when you know that He is victorious in the end and that makes you a winner.
♥ Freedom in Jesus is knowing He will sustain you even in times of trouble.
♥ Freedom in Jesus is the ability to forgive and love those who have hurt you.

There is no freedom when sin is prevalent in our lives. You will never experience true freedom until you surrender your life in obedience to Jesus Christ.

- ♥ Freedom in Jesus is knowing that when you are weak then He is strong.
- ♥ Freedom in Jesus is found when you trust Him completely.
- ♥ Freedom in Jesus is when you humbly look in the mirror and see God's beautiful creation.
- ♥ Freedom in Jesus is when you aren't fearful of the future, because you know He has a plan.
- ♥ Freedom in Jesus is when you lay down pride and worldliness.
- ♥ Freedom in Jesus is when you don't base who you are on what you have.
- ♥ Freedom in Jesus is when you don't judge others because of what they have or how they look.
- ♥ Freedom in Jesus is when you can share what God is doing in your life without fearing what others may think of you.

I think it's safe to say that everyone, everywhere wants to live a life of freedom. Free to choose your friends, your school, your leaders, your doctor, your religion, what you eat, etc. In fact, there are many areas in which we, especially in the United States, take our freedom for granted. Take a moment to list some situations in which you are free to make your own choice.

Desiring Freedom But Stuck in Sin!

The criminal who gets jail time as a penalty for his crime loses his freedom. The same can be said of Christians who lose their spiritual freedom because of sin. *"For everyone has sinned; all fall short of God's glorious standard"* (Romans 3:23). That's correct! We are all sinners. And when sin is not confessed, we become stuck in sin. When we are held captive by sin we then live in bondage. Where is the freedom? There is no freedom when sin is prevalent in our lives. You will never experience true freedom until you surrender your life in obedience to Jesus Christ. God's children are destined to be free!

Cherished

If we claim we have no sin, we are only fooling ourselves and not living in the truth. But if we confess our sins to him, he is faithful and just to forgive us our sins and to cleanse us from all wickedness.
—1 John 1:8–9

Amazing how such an ugly thing like sin can be so enticing! Has there been a time when you were stuck in sin? What was the lure? If you're honest, perhaps you would say that it looked really good from your vantage point. It wasn't until you were on the inside that "it" became ugly. Sometimes we begin to feel ugly on the inside because of the sin that has ensnared us. You've got it! This is one of Satan's greatest schemes. That's why he's called the great deceiver. The Bible tells us that Satan is like a snake in the grass or a thief in the night. However, we can't continue to use the age-old excuse, "The devil made me do it." No! We have to admit our wrong choices, choices that come with consequences. Choices that keep us from living a life of freedom!

Don't you realize that you become the slave of whatever you choose to obey? You can be a slave to sin, which leads to death, or you can choose to obey God, which leads to righteous living.
—Romans 6:16

The devil is like a spider who weaves her web for a meal ticket. Although the web is beautiful in its transparent design, it is a death trap for an unsuspecting insect carelessly traveling too close. Can you imagine the bondage of being caught in a spider's web? Much less the feeling of being zapped with a paralyzing stick, then rotated around and around in a gooey cocoon. Talk about claustrophobia!

It's the same feeling when you're caught in sin. I know. I've been there many times myself. When we stray into the path of disobedience, there will be painful consequences. So we've got to keep on the alert. The delicate web that Satan spins is sometimes hard to see at first. It is when life is going well that you become perfect prey. He's out to trip you up

♥

The delicate web that Satan spins is sometimes hard to see at first. It is when life is going well that you become perfect prey.

when you least expect it. Stay alert! Do you see how easy it is to become captivated by sin? To be wrapped up in bondage? Believe me, once the insect is being wound up in that sticky slime, it's way too late.

There is also another type of web, one with which we are all familiar. We have brought it into our homes. The Internet can be a good tool; however, if you aren't careful it can captivate you by all that it has to offer. When you sit at your computer, temptation is right in front of you; we're all just a click away from sin. Be careful! Don't be enticed and become its prey like so many.

Here are a few examples:

♥ You became curious and clicked on an inappropriate Web site. You said you would only look once, but you've gone back countless times hoping to see more.
♥ You shared gossip about a friend in an email, and it's been passed on to people you never intended to read it. Now, because of your guilt you've told lie after lie.
♥ You put an inappropriate picture of yourself online, and many have seen it. You don't want to face your peers because of your shame.
♥ You started gambling online and have secretly won a couple times. Now you wake up in the middle of the night to play your game in secret.

Have you fallen in the Web trap? Any regrets?

Shame and guilt are just two ways sin steals your freedom. And secrets—they can be dangerous! I'm not talking about keeping a birthday surprise. I'm talking about secret sins; secrets that keep you from living in freedom. Don't keep those secrets!

Do you recognize the battle raging in your heart and mind, good versus evil? You may be asking, "How do I keep all these darts from coming my way?" Let's continue our study by looking at another letter written by Paul. This time he is writing to his young friend, Timothy.

Cherished

♥
Shame and guilt are just two ways sin steals your freedom. And secrets— they can be dangerous!

Soldiers of Christ

In 2 Timothy, chapter 2, Paul encourages believers to endure the suffering they will encounter in this world. But he doesn't just leave us hanging in the depths of fear, instead he encourages us by saying, "And it's worth it! Keep on running the race." (author's paraphrase).

Read 2 Timothy 2:1–13.

What does it mean to be strong in grace? If you are a Christian, you are strong by Jesus's free gift of salvation, which is grace. It was Him alone who saved you. If you trust Jesus in every area of your life you will be strong in grace. (See Ephesians 2:8–9.)

So if it is strength you need, by grace God will provide you all the strength necessary. The next time you are in a battle with a friend, your parents, your thoughts, or something else, stop before you speak or make a move and call on Jesus. Those who are watching you will take note and see the wisdom in your actions.

> Example:
> *Battle*—struggle: a drawn-out conflict between adversaries, or against powerful forces (MSN Encarta Dictionary)

If you are going through a hard time, consider it a spiritual battle. You can go through the battle one of two ways. 1. You can choose to trust the Lord to get you through it and be *strong in grace*. 2. You can live in fear and doubt, because you have chosen to rely on your own strength. Whatever your battle, trust God to bring you through it.

Think back to a time when you experienced conflict with someone or perhaps you've experienced a lonely time and questioned your purpose.

Describe your emotions.

I've had a sense of lonliness and guilt and anger all at the same time

Describe your attitude.

All types of attitudes, Depending on the situation Probably bad

Describe how you responded to your crisis.

Can you see how trusting in God's grace when going through a negative circumstance can change the outcome?

Yes

As a believer (a Christian) you've been given the gift of God's grace. So the question is: Do you trust in God's grace or do you face your battles in your own strength?

I've been guilty of trying to face them with my own Strength. Working on that

Look at 2 Timothy 2:4–7 again.

Think about modern soldiers and what they must endure to be a good soldier.

What are some characteristics of a good soldier?

1.
2.
3.

What does it take to be a good athlete?

1.
2.
3.

What does it take to be a good farmer?

1.

2.

3.

A few words that came to my mind each time were:

- ♥ Commitment
- ♥ Training
- ♥ Goals

As a Christian soldier, what is your commitment?

What training have you had or are you pursuing at this time?

Do you have any spiritual goals? If you've never thought about it, now is a good time.

The goal is living your life in freedom for Jesus Christ.

Let's be honest. As Christ followers, we all could use a little more training. In fact, we should be in training for the rest of our lives. And about that goal—it's so easy to get our eyes off Jesus and into worldliness.

What Is the Goal?

The goal is living your life in freedom for Jesus Christ. Your eyes and heart are heaven-bound. Because you are so focused on Him in the race of life, you hear Him when He says go right or left. You know it is Him when you feel the need to stop, to rest, or to keep pressing on. You serve and love others because you really want to. You desire to reflect Him more and yourself less. The goal, simply put, is to be more like Jesus.

I don't know you personally, but today I can say it seems to me you're headed in the right direction! You're reading this Bible study, which was written to encourage you and help you stay on track or perhaps get you back on track or perhaps get you on track for the first time. You are studying God's Word and being receptive to His timeless truths. Perhaps now you are refocused and more ready than ever to apply His truths to your life.

By nothing less and nothing more we are justified by faith in Jesus Christ alone!

Soldiers are committed to their purpose. It is through the grace and power of God in us that we become obedient and willing soldiers of Jesus Christ.

Are you a soldier in the Lord's army? Will you step out when God calls you to? Will you go when He asks you to? Will you speak the truth when given the opportunity?

Read Ephesians 1:15–23.

I'd like to encourage you with this prayer for spiritual wisdom originally written by Paul to God's people in Ephesus. As you read it, imagine Paul praying this prayer for you. You can also model this prayer when praying for other believers. There is power in these words. There is power in prayer. Do you believe it?

When you read Paul's prayer, what words or statements did you find most encouraging? *Love for people everywhere. Wisdom. Understanding. Growth in knowledge. God's promise. Wonderful future. Power.* These are just a few that encouraged me. As Christians we can be encouraged by these words. God's power, the same power that raised Jesus from the dead, is at work in us. So from one soldier to another, don't be too hard on yourself. Instead, be encouraged!

Nowhere to Run!

Have you heard the story of Jonah? His story is as important today as it was around 2,800 years ago. It's amazing what God will do to keep His children from going in the wrong direction.

Read the Book of Jonah, chapter 1.

God told Jonah to travel to Nineveh and preach to the people there so they would turn from their wicked ways. Because Jonah feared the

Cherished

people of Nineveh and actually had hatred in his heart for them, he ran from God. When he got to the port of Joppa he found a ship that was getting ready to set sail to Tarshish, far from Nineveh. Once he was out at sea, God sent a storm. Not just any storm. This was a violent storm, and Jonah knew it was God trying to get his attention. Rather than bring harm to the other sailors on the boat, Jonah told them to throw him overboard. The men didn't want to be responsible for Jonah's death so they prayed first that God would not hold them accountable for taking Jonah's life. Then they threw him overboard.

Once Jonah was off the ship the sea grew calm. Waiting for Jonah at just the right time was a huge fish. The fish swallowed Jonah! I know it's crazy, but even crazier than that, Jonah actually lived in the fish's belly for three day and three nights. Talk about bondage. Jonah had nowhere to run, because God had him right where He wanted him, in the belly of a fish. Jonah probably spent a lot of time talking to God in the belly of that fish. He admitted he had been disobedient, he repented, and when he did the fish threw him up. Yuck! Don't you know he smelled so good! It's no surprise, sin is always messy.

Read chapters 2, 3, and 4 in the Book of Jonah for the rest of the story.

We can learn many lessons from Jonah's story.
- ♥ God will go to great lengths to get our attention.
- ♥ Jonah admits he is running from God. Repentance isn't just stepping out anywhere; it's running back to God.
- ♥ Jonah finally got the message and knew that God had shown him mercy. Spiritual discipline leads us to spiritual maturity.

God calls us to be obedient. Obedience shows that we trust God even when we don't understand what He is doing.

- ♥ Obey God when you don't want to.
- ♥ Obey God when you don't feel like it.
- ♥ Obey God when He first commands it.

I love the story of Jonah! What a great picture of God's love and compassion. We mess up so often, and each time God brings us back to Him one way or another. Sure, we are free to do things our own way. Yes, we are free to make our own choices. However, God always remains faithful even when we are disobedient.

What do you think was Jonah's main reason not to go to Nineveh? Do you think it had to do with selfish reasoning? Would it be so embarrassing or humiliating to go share God's message of repentance with these sinful people? Think about it. Why would Jonah not want the wicked people of Nineveh to experience the love and forgiveness of God? Was it because he thought these people deserved what they had coming to them? After all, these people were the enemies of God's people! In a self-righteous kind of way Jonah hoped God would destroy this powerful city. Jonah was a prophet. He loved God, but at one point he decided what *he* wanted was more important than what *God* wanted. Maybe he thought: *Sure, God, I'll serve you every day as long as it's something I want to do or if I can understand why you are having me do it.* This was a terrible mistake on Jonah's part, because God wants all people everywhere from every culture to repent and turn to Him. No matter how wicked, how sinful, God desires for everyone to trust in Him and be saved.

Have you ever felt angry, bitter, or hateful towards anyone or perhaps a certain group of people? Why did you have these feelings?

Do you see now that these people may be just the people God is commanding you to share His love with?

Why would it be hard to share Christ with this person or group of people?

If we really love God, then we will trust Him when He calls us to go and share His truth with others. That's huge! God forgives us when we don't obey. I don't know about you, but I pray that when God calls me or prompts me I won't wait, I won't run away, but I will be obedient right from the start.

It's unfortunate that we *will* fail and we *will* miss opportunities to share God's love. But isn't it good to know that even though we don't always love with a perfect love, God does? What an awesome thought! God is love so His love is perfect for you, for me, for everyone! This is good news! Through prayer, the Holy Spirit will remind us of His love and our hearts will be changed.

As we study the Book of Jonah we cannot help but recognize ourselves in his personal story. Loving God? Jonah loved God. But did He trust God? Not always. Love your neighbor? Well, it is clear that Jonah did not want to visit the people of Nineveh. Nor did he want to offer them the love and grace of God. He ran from God. He had hate in his heart for the people of Nineveh and would rather have given his life for the few sailors on the ship than for thousands who lived in Nineveh.

In light of Jonah's story, we should look at our own motives. We usually want to surround ourselves with people like us. People who talk like us, dress like us, live like us, and believe like us. And that's OK to an extent. As Christians we should enjoy having close friendships with those who are like-minded, those who are our brothers and sisters in Christ. However we should also desire to share God's love with those who do not know His love. Consider this: If we only hang out with people like us (whatever that means to you), then who will reach those who have never heard God's truth? Remember we were once without Christ too.

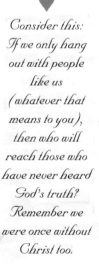

Consider this: If we only hang out with people like us (whatever that means to you), then who will reach those who have never heard God's truth? Remember we were once without Christ too.

What about you? Has there been a time when you turned the other way instead of doing what God prompted you to do? Maybe you acted like you didn't hear God?

♥ Disobedience will keep you stuck in sin.
♥ Obedience will lead you to freedom!
♥ The best way to describe bondage is SIN.
♥ If you are living in sin then you cannot live in freedom. Sin=bondage.

When we read Jonah, chapter 3, we see God had a purpose and it was much larger than just saving Jonah from the fish. Jonah couldn't see the big picture. Because of his disobedience he was missing God's blessing on his own life. Did you catch that? Disobedience is a blessing blocker! Finally, in chapter 3, Jonah fulfills his mission. The Lord gave Jonah a second chance and Jonah was obedient.

Has there been a time recently when you procrastinated or kept from doing what you knew you needed to do? What was the result and what have you learned from your mistake?

Despite Jonah's fear and bad attitude towards the evil people of Nineveh, God had a plan. He had prepared the hearts of the people to listen to the message Jonah would bring. God had mercy on the people of Nineveh and did not destroy them. Obedience freed Jonah from the fish; obedience saved Nineveh from destruction.

As you think about this story, pray and ask the Lord to show something new to you today. Perhaps you need some creative way to share God's truth with a person in your life. God probably won't have you swallowed up by a great fish but who knows what He will allow to make

♥

Talk about being cherished! Can you see how merciful God was to Jonah?

Cherished

it possible for someone to know His love, forgiveness, and grace. Don't stop the blessing. Be obedient when God calls you to go or when He calls you to stand up for something that is right. Most important, don't allow disobedience to bind you; instead, seek freedom through obedience.

Who Is God?

He is Creator, our heavenly Father, Abba, Master, Yahweh, Prince of Peace, Alpha and Omega, Everlasting God. He is my friend, my shelter, the great I Am. He is Jehovah Rophe (the Lord who heals), Jehovah Nissi (our Banner), Jehovah Jireh (the Lord who provides), our Shepherd, Judge, God our Rock, Strength, Messiah, Wonderful Counselor, God our everything! God is love!

List other names of God from the Bible.

He is not just *a* God; He is *the* God of the whole universe. Yes, He cherishes you and me! And also the frailest child, the one who is an alcoholic, the one who is an outcast, the one who is sick, the one who is lonely, the one who is hungry, the one who is weak, the one who is strong, the richest and the poorest, the one who is guilty, the one who is troubled, the one who is depressed, the one who is _____. God's love is greater and stretches farther than our mind can conceive. His love is deep. His love is wide. And yet you can call Him "Abba Father."

Talk about being cherished! Can you see how merciful God was to Jonah? Do you recognize the love and compassion He had for him? God went to extremes for the people of Nineveh. He didn't just walk away and say, "Oh well, I guess I can't use Jonah." No. Instead, He stopped him from running. He didn't let him drown. He used Jonah in spite of his selfishness and disobedience. And in the end all things worked according to His plan.

Jonah ran, but he couldn't hide from God. Finally, in the belly of a large fish, God had his full attention. Jonah repented of his sin and went in the direction God was leading him. He was obedient in the end. He was blessed in the end. Many were saved in the end. It's hard to imagine all of this from a man who ran from God.

What about you? Have you been disobedient? Are you running from God?

Can you see that God will go to all kinds of extremes to get your attention?

Have you experienced His discipline? Write your story and share it with someone.

So, if you continue to be drawn to a certain sin or two, turn around, run for your life; seek freedom. Run away from sin and run into the loving arms of God!

How does God's discipline bring us to spiritual freedom? Write your thoughts and pray that the Lord will discipline you and draw you closer to Him. Pray that you will not miss His blessing.

Read Hebrews 12:10–11.

These two verses teach us the purpose of God's discipline. He does it for our good; He does it to produce a harvest of righteousness. He pursues us by any means necessary, because He loves us.

And Speaking of Fish...

Have you ever seen a sucker fish? If you have I'm guessing it was either sucking garbage off the rocks at the bottom of the fish aquarium or sucking slime from the side of the glass walls. Nasty stuff is what the sucker fish craves! Sounds like sin to me. Unless we turn away from it quick, we'll continue to crave it until it consumes us...garbage! When you choose sin over obedience to God there will be consequences that you *will* endure. Just remember you can't blame God. You can't blame Satan. You have to take full responsibility. So, if you continue to be drawn to a certain sin or two, turn around, run for your life; seek freedom. Run away from sin and run into the loving arms of God!

What About You? Are You Running?

Today many girls are running but have no clue in what direction they are headed. If this is you, stop! Seek God. In your heart and mind sin creates the opposite of freedom—slavery and bondage. Guard your heart, fight for it. It is the place where girls battle discontentment everyday; where jealousy becomes the fiery dart that robs them of joy; a place where girls who desire both physical and spiritual purity often lose the battle, simply because they want to be loved and accepted at any cost. Give your heart to One who cherishes you and who is strong enough to protect you. God wants to give you His love. *"And hope does not disappoint us, because God has poured out his love into our hearts by the Holy Spirit, whom he has given us"* (Romans 5:5 NIV). Do you see it? God fills our hearts with His love!

Recognize the type of battle you are fighting. Call upon the name of the Lord your God. Hold on to Him and His truth, not the temporary trends of this world.

Read Ephesians 6:10–18.

As a Christian, ask God to give you a deeper desire to read and memorize Scripture. When you do you'll begin to pray about everything as you enjoy a sweet relationship with Him. Only then will you experience spiritual freedom, win the battle, and live victoriously.

For we are not fighting against flesh-and-blood enemies, but against evil rulers and authorities of the unseen world, against mighty powers in this dark world and against evil spirits in the heavenly places.
—Ephesians 6:12

After reading this session have you identified areas in your life that are holding you captive? Give these areas to Jesus. Ask Him to win the battles in your life. He wants you to live in freedom. Don't allow Satan to rob you of joy any longer. If you're a Christian, Satan cannot have authority over you, but he can do a pretty good job at intimidating you—keeping you tangled up in fear and preventing you from experiencing the freedom God desires for you.

How do I know this? *"It is for freedom that Christ has set us free. Stand firm, then, and do not let yourselves be burdened again by a yoke of slavery"* (Galatians 5:1 NIV). If there is anything going on in your heart that is keeping you from freedom, memorize and pray and say out loud this verse: *"The one who is in you is greater than the one who is in the world"* (1 John 4:4 NIV). Trust Jesus.

My Prayer

Father God, I pray that my beautiful sister will find freedom in Your amazing grace. Lord, I pray You would help her experience Your presence like rain washing over her, setting her free from sin, secrets, hurts, and fear. I pray that today would be the day that she receives Your gift of grace and unending love if she has not already done so. Lord, may she come to You boldly knowing that she is cherished and loved by You. Thank You in advance for all You are doing in her life. In Jesus's name I pray, amen.

Cherished

GAB Session
~ with Chandra ~

Finding Freedom in the Midst of Garbage

Recently I was invited to minister in Cairo, Egypt. What a blessing that my husband, Bruce, and my daughters, Lindsey and Holly, had the opportunity to travel with me. The purpose of the trip was to glorify God through the teaching of His Word and by showing His love to the people we would meet. God opened many doors of ministry during our 15-day visit; it was amazing! We encouraged the hurting, the needy, and the poor. We shared God's Word with the Maadi Community Church family, and they, in return, blessed us. We were hosted by sisters and brothers in Christ whom we had never met, yet it seemed as if we had known them forever. One family opened their home to us and took care of our every need. Their love for Jesus Christ was evident in the way they served our family. It's so good to be a part of the family of God!

We saw the pyramids, the temples, the museums, and had dinner on a felucca on the Nile River; however one place that touched our hearts like no other was Mokattam. Also known as Garbage City, this is a community where many Christians live because the Egyptian government allows them to work there to recycle garbage. It's unfortunate that those who are born in Garbage City will most likely live there the rest of their life. It's a cycle that has repeated itself generation after generation. Young girls who live there will most likely be married there, raise their families there, and work there. Although the suffering is great, those who proclaim to be Christians find their hope in Jesus Christ the same way that Christians do all over the world.

As we drove down the narrow, garbage-filled roads our first reaction was to feel sorry for these people because of their living conditions. They live, eat, play, and work in the midst of garbage, flies, and everything else that the trucks dump. However, after a little while we began to see children running and laughing as they played freely, chasing a ball they had made out of paper. We saw men visiting as they sat in chairs that had once been in someone's living room. The women were looking through the garbage piles searching for fabrics and other items they could recycle. These recycled items earn them income, so they can feed and afford shelter for their family. Occasionally they run across something really good like an old coffee pot that works but was no longer the right color for someone's kitchen. You know what they say? One man's junk is another man's treasure. When we looked at their faces, it didn't appear that anyone was complaining or unhappy; instead it seemed that they had joy in the midst of their suffering.

While in Garbage City we were fortunate to spend some time holding babies in the orphanage. There was a sweet spirit in that tiny, dimly lit room as the Holy Spirit filled us with His love, which we freely gave to those precious children. What a humbling sight for me to see my daughters and my husband hold and play with these children; some with deformities or mental problems, while others seemed perfectly normal. My eyes filled with tears because I knew the Lord had planned this precious moment long before we ever thought about visiting Egypt. The Father's love is amazing and His timing is perfect!

As Christ followers, we have been given the Spirit of God's Son in our hearts, and we are His heirs, His sons and daughters (Galatians 4:6–7). Isn't that beautiful? To think that all that is His belongs to His children. Hey...that's me! I don't know about you, but I'm sure glad I am an heir of God!

Our trip to Egypt was a once-in-a-lifetime opportunity. I'm thankful to God for the time we spent in Cairo and for the spiritual growth that has come from this experience. After returning to my home in Texas instead of thinking so much about what I want, I've been more grateful for what I have. Instead of thinking about my next big purchase, I'm thinking about what I can give away. Instead of thinking about my needs, I've thought more about the needs of others. And my love for others...well, lets just say it has more meaning than ever before.

Cherished

The next time you are near a world globe, maybe in your world geography class, place your finger on the map where you live. You will quickly see how tiny you are and how huge the world really is. And to think God loves *everyone everywhere*! (John 3:16) What a good reminder that God is a big GOD!

Finding Peace in the Midst of Suffering

Our guide through the Egyptian community that day was Nathan, a 24-year-old missionary who loves and cares deeply for these people. God has given him a passion to serve them. He lives with them, walks with them, eats with them, and plays with them. Most important, he shares Jesus with them. Nathan told us, though it's hard to explain, that when you depend on God for every meal, where you lay your head down at night, and for whatever you need tomorrow, you find rest and peace of mind. Ultimately you experience true freedom. You don't worry because you trust God will take care of your every need. What a testimony! What a beautiful example of one who knows that when we do the right things with the right motives, there's no limit to what God will do in our lives!

> *And since we are his children, we are his heirs. In fact, together with Christ we are heirs of God's glory. But if we are to share his glory, we must also share his suffering.*
> —Romans 8:17

My experience in Egypt reminded me that no matter where we live we will all go through times of suffering in this life. Our suffering may look different than others, but it's how we go through it that changes us. Those who choose faith in Jesus Christ and live life sold out to Him can experience freedom even in the midst of this suffering! I would have never imagined anyone would choose to live in Garbage City until I met Nathan. This young man earns only a small income from his ministry, always has enough to give to others, and is so intoxicated with his freedom in Christ that he continues to crave more.

Ask God to save you. Trust in His grace.

When we read about Paul in the Bible we see that he suffered beatings, shipwrecks, and prison (2 Corinthians 11:16–33). The people of Mokattam find their suffering in the midst of Garbage City. Where is your place of suffering? Or perhaps you have yet to experience suffering in your life. I pray what you've just read will prepare you for suffering when it comes, and you too will find freedom in the midst of your circumstance.

Have you chosen Jesus? If not, you can right now. Don't wait. Have you chosen freedom? If not, you can walk in freedom and find warmth in the shelter of His love today. Have you chosen love? God is love, and He loves you right where you are!

If you confess with your mouth that Jesus is Lord and believe in your heart that God raised him from the dead, you will be saved. For it is by believing in your heart that you are made right with God, and it is by confessing with your mouth that you are saved.
—Romans 10:9–10

Ask God to save you. Trust in His grace. You may choose to pray a prayer of faith like this one:

Heavenly Father, I recognize that I am a sinner and repent of my sin. Thank You for sending Jesus to die on the Cross to pay the penalty for my sin once and for all. Thank You that Your grace is free; it cost me nothing because Jesus paid my debt. My desire is to live by the example of Your Son and my Savior, Jesus Christ. I believe that by grace I have been saved and through faith, accepting this free gift, I have eternal life. I celebrate today knowing that I have new life starting this moment. Thank You for saving me. Thank you for setting me free from the bondage of sin. Thank You for loving me this much. Amen.

The Bible tells us in Romans 6:14 about our new condition in Jesus: *"Sin is no longer your master, for you no longer live under the requirements of the law. Instead you live under the freedom of God's grace."*

Cherished

My Journal

Choose Jesus—Choose Freedom—Choose Love. Do these words take on new meaning for you now that you've studied them more in this session? Write down your thoughts on each statement.

Choose Jesus. ～～～～～～～～～～～～～～～～～～～～
～～～～～～～～～～～～～～～～～～～～～～～～～～
～～～～～～～～～～～～～～～～～～～～～～～～～～
～～～～～～～～～～～～～～～～～～～～～～～～～～

Choose Freedom. ～～～～～～～～～～～～～～～～～～
～～～～～～～～～～～～～～～～～～～～～～～～～～
～～～～～～～～～～～～～～～～～～～～～～～～～～
～～～～～～～～～～～～～～～～～～～～～～～～～～

Choose Love. ～～～～～～～～～～～～～～～～～～～～
～～～～～～～～～～～～～～～～～～～～～～～～～～
～～～～～～～～～～～～～～～～～～～～～～～～～～
～～～～～～～～～～～～～～～～～～～～～～～～～～
～～～～～～～～～～～～～～～～～～～～～～～～～～

Cherished

Love the Lord Your God More

"You must love the Lord your God with all your heart, all your soul, and all your mind."
—Matthew 22:37

Have you ever been around someone who acts like they know everything? Have you ever said "Yes!" under your breath when someone corrected them or put them in their place? That doesn't sound very nice, I know, but because of our nature we secretly smile and feel a little less stupid when the big shot is corrected, especially in public. This is how I imagine the onlookers feeling the day Jesus was questioned by the "big shots" in Jerusalem.

Read Matthew 22:1–14.

Jesus is telling the parable of the wedding feast, while being challenged by religious leaders. He puts the focus on His Kingdom as He tells a parable inviting all those listening to be *His* guest at *His* banquet. Although this was a message of love, the religious leaders were too prideful to receive it. They were tripped up by their own man-made laws and ideas.

God loves us so much that He extends His invitation to us over and over. Have you accepted His invitation? If not, what are you waiting for? Jesus is inviting you today—right now, this very moment—to enter into a love relationship with Him. With that comes salvation, forgiveness of

♥
God loves us so much that He extends His invitation to us over and over. Have you accepted His invitation? If not, what are you waiting for?

sin, a new heart, a new beginning, and eternal life. Talk about freedom!

However, you have a choice to make. Looking back to Matthew 22:11, will you be like the guest who rejects Him or will you receive the invitation and slip into the wedding garment He presents—clothes of righteousness? *"Everyone who calls on the name of the LORD shall be saved"* (Romans 10:13).

How does this parable apply to your life today?

Funny how people of all cultures have developed different ideas for what they should do to please God when in fact Jesus has already told us that He is the way, the truth, and the life (John 14:6). It's not a secret! The answers people come up with are just that, man-made. Hello! That is called *religion* but God desires for all people to experience a growing *relationship* with Him through Jesus Christ. It's who we know (Jesus) that changes us, *not* what *we do*.

What are some man-made rules that some Christians follow today?

Jesus is inviting you today— right now, this very moment— to enter into a love relationship with Him.

Once we surrender our lives to Jesus our actions begin to reflect Him. We *hear* the Word *then* we become *doers* of the Word. It all begins in the heart.

The "Big Shots" Try to Trap Jesus

Read Matthew 22:15–22.

The Pharisees, a religious group, and the Herodians, a political party for governor Herod, were determined to trip up Jesus with a question. While normally these two groups despised each other, they teamed up and developed a plan to trap Jesus. Although they didn't agree on much, both the Pharisees and the Herodians wanted to see Jesus arrested. So they asked this seemingly tough question about paying taxes. Jesus knew exactly what they were scheming and gave them an answer that I'm sure left them speechless and embarrassed.

Picture this: A bully is teasing his victim and suddenly feels a tap on his shoulder. He turns around and in an instant is single-handedly picked up by some Arnold Schwarzenegger-type and slammed in the face with a cherry pie. OK…got the picture? These dudes got what was coming to them, but in a Jesus kind of way.

Read Matthew 22:23–32.

Now the Sadducees wanted their turn at trapping Jesus. Boy, do these guys have the wrong focus. They just don't get it! I love how Jesus responds to their strange question in verses 29–32. Once again Jesus put them in their place. Humbled, I'd hope.

> *"You are in error because you do not know the Scriptures or the power of God. At the resurrection people will neither marry nor be given in marriage; they will be like the angels in heaven. But about the resurrection of the dead—have you not read what God said to you, 'I am the God of Abraham, the God of Isaac, and the God of Jacob'? He is not the God of the dead but of the living."*
> —Matthew 22:29–32 (NIV)

Verse 33 tells us, *"When the crowds heard this, they were astonished at this teaching."*

The reason they were astonished is most likely because they too did not know Scripture. If we as Christians, who know God, would read and study Scripture more often we wouldn't be so surprised when God works in our circumstances. What a great reminder that we need to study the Scriptures. These people had front row seats to hear Jesus. Let's hope some went home and became better students of the Scriptures.

What about you? Are you in shock or in awe when God works in your life and in those around you? There is a difference. The one in shock responds in disbelief! The one in awe praises Him and is amazed at His glory.

Think back to a time when you were shocked or in awe at what God did. Or maybe you have known others who experienced God's miracle, and they were in shock.

Someone in shock may respond like this: "No way! What? Are you serious? I can't believe it!"

Someone in awe might have this response: "God, thank You for answering my prayer; You are wonderful!"

Or maybe your experience was a silent moment of appreciation when you enjoyed a beautiful sunset or sunrise. Can you see the difference between shock and awe?

Journal about a time when you were in awe of God's wonder.

What's Really Important

OK, let's continue. The story gets even better!

The Jewish religious leaders had come up with hundreds of laws and regulations covering any and everything you can imagine. They claimed the people had to live by these rules and regulations in order to do the *one thing* that was most important in life—obeying God. By obeying God they believed a person would then experience His blessings. For generations, the religious leaders debated which of all the laws was the most important to keep, and they hadn't come up with an absolutely agreed-upon answer.

So the Pharisees got together and tried to stump Jesus again. An expert in the law asked Him, "What is the greatest commandment?"

Jesus replied: "'Love the Lord your God with all your heart and with all your soul and with all your mind.' This is the first and greatest commandment. And the second is like it: 'Love your neighbor as yourself.' All the Law and the Prophets hang on these two commandments."
—Matthew 22:37–40 (NIV)

This is Jesus Himself telling us what is of greatest importance to God. Wow! Take a minute to get up and look at yourself in the mirror. Repeat Matthew 22:37–40 out loud. Now say "(your name), this is important to God!"

When Jesus gave His answer He was quoting Deuteronomy 6:5 and Leviticus 19:18. Needless to say, the Pharisees were stunned when Jesus answered their question with something they already knew. The problem is they "knew" it in their *mind* but not necessarily in their *heart*.

Think about life, your life. You should love God with everything you are. Do whatever it takes to love Him first. This means putting your selfish desires away. You need to devote yourself to understanding Him—to deepening your relationship with Him. Challenge yourself and others to put Him first.

Getting Serious

Let us look a little deeper into what it means to love God with all your heart, all your soul, and all your mind.

Your heart

"For where your treasure is, there your heart will be also."
—Matthew 6:21 (NIV)

"The good man out of the good treasure of his heart brings forth what is good; and the evil man out of the evil treasures brings forth what is evil; for his mouth speaks from that which fills his heart."
—Luke 6:45 (NASB)

Since, then, you have been raised with Christ, set your heart on things above, where Christ is seated at the right hand of God.
—Colossians 3:1 (NIV)

Truly our heart is the wellspring of life. Have you taken the time to evaluate your heart lately? What does it reflect? What do you treasure?

Your soul

Everyone has a soul. We all will live forever in heaven or hell. Our response to Jesus in this life determines our eternal state. "What good will it be for a man if he gains the whole world, yet forfeits his soul? Or what can a man give in exchange for his soul?"
—Matthew 16:26 (NIV)

Your mind

Set your mind on things above, not on earthly things.
—Colossians 3:2 (NIV)

Therefore, prepare your minds for action; be self-controlled, set your hope fully in the grace to be given you when Jesus Christ is revealed. As obedient children, do not conform to the evil desires you had when you lived in ignorance.
—1 Peter 1:13–14 (NIV)

Truly our heart is the wellspring of life. Have you taken the time to evaluate your heart lately? What does it reflect? What do you treasure?

Cherished

How can we do these things?

♥ Surrender our lives to Him.
♥ Pray.
♥ Study His Word.
♥ Worship Him.
♥ Seek wise counsel from other Christians in the church.
♥ Serve Him.

Maybe you have put your friends first, your boyfriend, or just "stuff." The way you become best friends with someone is by spending lots of time with her. You talk on the phone, text, Facebook, Myspace. Some of you may spend hours of your day talking to a friend. Think about it. Write it down. How many times have you talked to your best friend today?

For some of you, it's not a friend or friends; it is a video game or the couch. Yes. That's right. Because you are bored you find yourself on the couch *a lot*. I know; I have two daughters and I was once a teenager too.

The next time you are bored or realize you have watched way too much reality TV, get up! Get your Bible and find a place where you can focus on God. Talk with Him. Tell Him your troubles. Tell Him you love Him. Share your thoughts with Him. Or just be still and let Him speak to you. By spending time with God you will discover His priceless love for you and begin to understand what it means to love the Lord with all your heart.

Take the Challenge

Every day this week, find time in your busy schedule to sit and meet with God. Ask the Lord to purge your heart of anything that you have put before Him.

How well do you know Scripture, God's Word?

Has reading the Bible changed your relationship with God? How?

Has it changed the way you live your life or not?

Write down some obvious changes in your life since you gave your life to Jesus Christ.

Are there some areas that need to change?

Thoughts:

Yes my thoughts need to change!

Actions:

Yes Actions need to change!!

Attitude:

My attitude definitely needs to change each and everyday

Love for others:

Definitely need more love for others!

Investigate my life, O God, find out everything about me; Cross-examine and test me, get a clear picture of what I'm about; See for yourself whether I've done anything wrong—then guide me on the road to eternal life.

—Psalm 139:23–24 (*The Message*)

Simply His Power

The religious leaders and educators of that day had the wrong focus. They were trying to earn God's love and His favor by following all sorts of rules. No different from today, some were trying to be the most intelligent. They enjoyed it when others had the perception that they were intellects of religion. They felt comfortable on the pedestal people placed them on. They liked the fact that the common villager felt lower than them. Sadly, their pride and cocky attitude would get them nowhere in the end.

This isn't a thing of the past—this still happens today! I sometimes wonder why it's easier for some people to believe Satan's lies rather than having a simple childlike faith and believing Jesus is who He says He is. We have the answer. Why do we make it so hard?

The more God-centered your life is, the more you will know His blessings and the stronger He'll make you when facing life's problems. The deeper your relationship and commitment to Him grow, the deeper your love for Him and others will become. It's simple, right? Well, it might sound simple but...

It's impossible to love God with everything we are—impossible to express love unselfishly to others. As hard as we might try, we simply fall short. So, what's the bottom line? *God has to be this work of love in you.* It is He who enables you to do what He says you should do. It is only through His love that you can love Him and love others and learn to love yourself.

Very powerful !!

Commit your way to the LORD; trust him and he will do this: He will make your righteousness shine like the dawn, the justice of your cause like the noonday sun.
—Psalm 37:5–6 (NIV)

His Love is Greater

Read John 14:1–3.

"Don't let your hearts be troubled. Trust in God, now trust also in me. There is more than enough room in my Father's home. If this were not so, would I have told you that I am going to prepare a place for you? When everything is ready, I will come and get you, so that you will always be with me where I am."

As a believer I can't wait to see what He has prepared for me in heaven!

Who is saying this? Jesus. Jesus made us this promise. As a believer I can't wait to see what He has prepared for me in heaven! Days filled with worship, sweet fellowship with loved ones, streets of gold. Mansions! No tears, no sorrow. Not to mention seeing Jesus face-to-face every moment! You have to want it! Whew! Just talking about it gets me so excited!

These verses just begin to give us a glimpse of God's great and empowering love for us. Jesus wants us to be with Him. Forever. Amazing!

You may have heard these promises many times. The question is, do you believe them? If you said, "Yes!" this should reflect in the way you live your life. If you said, "Umm, I don't know; I'm not sure," this will also reflect in the way you live your life. There is no freedom in wondering where you will spend eternity. If you are unsure, you are choosing to live life without peace and joy in your heart. Choose Jesus today!

Read John 14:4–6.

"I am the way and the truth and the life. No one comes to the Father except through me. If you really knew me, you would know my Father as well. From now on, you do know him and have seen him."
—John 14:6–7 (NIV)

Cherished

The disciples walked with Him, ate with Him, went on the road with Him, and still they didn't get it. Thomas's question in John 14:5 clearly indicates that. But Jesus patiently answers him in simple, straightforward language. Don't you know the Lord does the same with us? He continues to be patient with His children. He continues to show His love and mercy to us even in times of doubt and questioning. He continues to pursue His children. He never gives up on you. He cherishes you! His love never fails.

Read John 14:7–29

Even after Jesus's answer in verses 6 and 7, Philip asks another question. And Jesus again answers in love. I get so excited when I read this! To know the Father loves you and me so much. *"You can ask for anything in my name, and I will do it, so that the Son can bring glory to the Father"* (John 14:13). Over and over in the Bible, He gives direction, truth, and forgiveness. Over and over and over He says He wants to have this glorious, wonderful relationship with us. He continues to pour out His love over you. His pursuit is relentless. Through His Word, through people, through His creation, through the still, small voice that you hear in the midst of this crazy busy world, He never stops because He loves you!

Maybe you are saying…Chandra, OK, I get it and guess what? I already love Him. That's great! But do you love Him by trusting Him? Not only with your eternal salvation, which is a pretty huge thing to trust Him for, but do you trust Him with your daily life? Do you obey Him in the little things each day? He has given us His Spirit, the Counselor; His Spirit enables us to obey Him. When you say, "I love the Lord my God with all my heart, mind, and soul," that means that you trust Him. Our love and trust is measured in our obedience. Jesus said, *"All who love me will do what I say"* (John 14:23).

Wow! Our love & trust is measured in our obedience!!

Read Deuteronomy 28:1–14.

To enjoy God's blessings, we trust and obey. Throughout the Scripture, the Lord tells of His blessings for obedience. Jeremiah 17:7 says, *"Blessed are those who trust in the LORD and have made the LORD their hope and confidence."*

The LORD will establish you as his holy people, as he promised you on oath, if you keep the commands of the LORD your God and walk in his ways…The LORD will open the heavens, the storehouse of his bounty, to send rain on your land in season and to bless all the work of your hands…. However, if you do not obey the LORD your God and do not carefully follow all his commands and decrees I am giving you today, all these curses will come upon you and overtake you.
—Deuteronomy 28:9, 12, 15 (NIV)

If you can, take the time to read all of chapter 28. The blessings are so awesome and the curses…well, let's just say, for me and my house we will serve the Lord. We get to choose. Obedience or disobedience? Blessings or curses?

God will allow us to come face-to-face with pain and struggle, sometimes even death in order *"that we would not trust in ourselves, but in God who raises the dead"* (2 Corinthians 1:9 NASB).

Read the story of Elijah, a person just like you who truly loved God with all his heart, mind, and soul (see 1 Kings 17:1–24). Like Elijah, you may have times of loneliness, but you are never alone. Like Elijah, you may question God, but He hears your cries. Elijah prayed believing God would answer and bring the boy back to life. A great miracle occurred that day. Elijah showed great faith in God. He was desperate and knew he could do nothing—but he trusted God could work in any situation.

What About You?

Are you willing to place your complete faith in God? Even when your circumstances seem impossible, God will use that time to strengthen your faith. Perhaps there is something you are going through now. So what about it?

Will you put your complete faith and trust in God? Write down your thoughts or concerns.

So what about it? Will you put your complete faith and trust in God?

Cherished

Wow, this truly hit home with me. It seems I am getting deeper & deeper over my head with Jenna. I truly have to trust that God will get us thru this & help Jenna get well in all areas. I truly feel like I have a living baby doll !!

When you pray do you trust God to answer your prayer?

That's an interesting one. I think I do, hopefully.

Ask God to send the rain in the midst of your pain, to wash over you an abundance of forgiveness, peace, and joy. Jesus wants us to forsake our idolatry and return to Him and love Him with a full heart. Because of His unending love and grace for you He wants you to experience a life filled with peace and joy. I encourage you to ask God to give you a heart of faith, to love Him with your whole heart, and to become a sold-out, committed, contagious Christian.

Do you want life as God intended life to be lived? Choose to love the Lord God with all your heart, soul, and mind. Believe that He is the one and only living God, full of grace, truth, and life. His name is Jesus, the one and only Savior of the world.

Take some time to write out your thoughts or your desires on how you can love God more.

I so want to give everything over to God. There is so much to "worry" about in this life and I HAVE to have HIM to lean on and trust we will get thru this !!

Write out a prayer to God as though you are writing Him a letter.

Dear Lord,

I just want to do everything for you ! I want a closer walk with You. I want that tight relationship you long for. I know you will help me thru everything I encounter and deal with daily !

"Let your light shine before men, that they may see your good deeds and praise your Father in heaven."
—Matthew 5:16 (NIV)

Read Psalm 110:1; Matthew 22:41–46; John 8:58; and John 10:30.

Who do you say Jesus is? This is life's most important question. It's not about your denomination, how you were brought up, or what your parents believe. All other theological questions are secondary when considering the identity of Jesus Christ.

The most important act of obedience God requires of us is this: to believe in His Son. In John 6:29 Jesus says, *"This is the only work God wants from you: Believe in the one he has sent."*

We must believe that Jesus is God.

In the beginning the Word already existed. The Word was with God, and the Word was God.
—John 1:1

We proclaim to you the one who existed from the beginning , whom we have heard and seen. We saw him with our own eyes and touched him with our own hands. He is the Word of life. The one who is life itself was revealed to us, and we have seen him. And now we testify and proclaim to you that he is the one who is eternal life. He was with the Father, and then he was revealed to us. We proclaim to you what we ourselves have actually seen and heard so that you may have fellowship with us. And our fellowship is with the Father and with his Son, Jesus Christ. We are writing these things so that you may fully share our joy.
—1 John 1:1–4

When John wrote this letter, much like our world today, believers were compromising their faith by living and looking more like the world instead of leading a godly lifestyle. John's letter was written to be a

♥

Who do you say Jesus is? This is life's most important question.

wake-up call for the church. He encouraged them to return to God, reminding them of the joy they would experience.

As you see it, in what ways have Christians today lost their commitment?

They compromise way too much

In what areas do you think you look more like the world than Jesus Christ? *I'm no exception, I also compromise on things*

In those areas that look more like the world, how can you get back on track?

By studying the word, more fellowship with other believers.

♥
Remember, there is only one way to enter the kingdom of God— through Jesus Christ. You must have the proper wedding clothes—His righteousness.

Reflect back to the wedding parable at the beginning of our study (Matthew 22). Remember the guest who didn't wear the proper wedding clothes? He was thrown out. Why? Because by his actions he was saying, "I don't need you. I can do it my way, because I like my way better." What about you? Are you choosing to wear the clothes of righteousness, the ones Jesus provides for His wedding guests or are you selfishly rejecting them and doing life your way? Maybe that still, small voice in your heart began to beat faster and faster when you read this story. Remember, there is only one way to enter the kingdom of God— through Jesus Christ. You must have the proper wedding clothes—His righteousness.

Let me take this moment to speak the truth in love. If you are trying to get right with God on your own terms, then you too are choosing *not* to love God with all your heart, soul, and mind. You're refusing to trust

God completely. Maybe you are still depending on you—your timing, your path, your knowledge, your way. Maybe you have chosen a side-to-side relationship with Jesus instead of a face-to-face one.

Side-to-side relationship: "Lord, I want you here, but let's discuss things before I make the final decision."

Face-to-face relationship: intimate, surrender; You want nothing more than to reflect Him in all your choices.

Why are we so stubborn sometimes? How can we choose our own way when we know disobedience leads us down a path of destruction and grief? I pray after reading this session you will choose the path of obedience, which is the path to blessing. There's no question, God's plan is so much better than our own.

Purify Our Hearts

When dry beans are cooking on a stovetop the beans that aren't good float to the top. Has the Holy Spirit used this session to stir up your heart, bringing some of the "not so good stuff" to the top? When you think about it, it's really a good thing. God is working to purify your heart. He's growing you up spiritually!

List some of the "not so good stuff" that needs to be taken out of your heart.

Bitterness
Depression
Attitude - stubbornness
Pride

Sometimes, even though you may see the bad stuff, you stubbornly decide to leave it there, or you just ignore it. I'm praying for you, my sister, that you would deal with these things now before they boil over and make a mess of your life.

Take some time to write down your thoughts or perhaps your struggles. *I struggle daily with bitterness. There's times when my attitude definitely gets in the way of choosing what God would have me do.*

Remember, heroes of the faith like Paul, Moses, and David messed up in life. So many people in the Bible went through hard times. God never abandoned them, and He won't abandon you.

A Masterpiece in Progress

Wow! I just have to say this study has challenged me! God really worked on my heart as I prepared these two sessions. He is growing me, and I pray He is growing you. During this study did you ever feel like the daughter who had disappointed her Father? Me too! I felt unworthy to be His child. But once again, our faithful, loving Father spoke to me in His Word. Look at the passage He immediately led me to so I could share it with you. We don't need to stay in a defeated state of mind.

> *For if you listen and don't obey, it is like glancing at your face in a mirror. You see yourself, walk away, and forget what you look like. But if you look carefully into the perfect law that sets you free, and if you do what it says and don't forget what you heard, then God will bless you for doing it.*
> —James 1:23–25

We are each a unique and beautiful masterpiece, and God, the Creator of the canvas, continues to refine our beauty with each brushstroke.

God sure knows me well. If I look in a mirror and see something out of place, I will surely try my best to fix it. I take this verse as a wonderful reminder that we are a work in progress. If we don't study His Word, then we might never look at our heart to notice its imperfections. He blesses us with His Word, shows us our sins, and tells us how to live, all so we can obey and be in a position for Him to bless us. We are each a unique and beautiful masterpiece, and God, the Creator of the canvas, continues to refine our beauty with each brushstroke.

God, who began the good work within you, will continue his work until it is finally finished on the day when Christ Jesus returns.
—Philippians 1:6

My Prayer

O Father, that I would turn my ways over to You, that I would be found faithful in doing Your will. When I look into the mirror deep in my heart let me see the speck that is keeping me from a face-to-face relationship with You. What a treasure You are! More valuable than anything I could purchase or desire. You alone, Lord! If I have been misled by worldliness, Lord, get me back on track. If Satan is using past hurt, ungodly friends, disappointment, and low self-image to keep me from You, today I ask You to shine the light on that speck and remove it so I can see Your path more clearly. Lord, right now cleanse me from all my sin. Help me to lay down my selfish pride and become like putty in Your hand. Mold me, shape me, and Lord, begin this new work in me today! Father, my greatest desire is to love You with all my heart, mind, and soul. Amen.

Cherished

GAB Session
~ with Chandra ~

Stay On Track!

Last winter we joined our dear friends at their Colorado mountain place. They had told us for years how wonderful cross-country skiing is and that we really must try it. We were hesitant.

Why? Well, the last time I went snow skiing I was trying something new when I hurt myself. Trust me...eight inches of fresh powder may look beautiful, but it can be dangerous too! I'd skied many times before that but never in powder. I thought surely it would be easier with more fluff to break my fall. Instead, I tripped over the snow and sprained my ankle. Yep. It was real pretty! My first thought was, "How am I going to get off this mountain?" Although I trust my husband Bruce completely I immediately got a picture in my mind of me leaning on his back, skis on his, screaming at him, him screaming back at me causing a scene the whole way down the mountain. So we both agreed that it would be better if Bob helped me down. Although Bruce is a very good skier, our friend Bob has skied more often in powder.

Now you have to get this picture in your mind: Bob is probably five foot nine, 150 pounds with me on his back. I'm five foot four, and I won't give the other information. Thankfully, we got down the mountain and I vowed to never ski again. Poor Bob was probably relieved! So now you can understand the reason behind my hesitation about going cross-country skiing. It was, however, a beautiful day so I thought I'd at least give it a try.

We went to the warming house to get our equipment, and the guy behind the counter asked if I had ever cross-country skied before. When I said, "No," he didn't gasp and make me fearful; instead, he patiently got me set up with beginner's equipment. He took me out and gave me some instructions on how to put on my equipment correctly. You could tell he was confident and passionate about cross-county skiing. He was obviously knowledgeable about it because he gives private lessons, has classes, and runs the ski shop. I'd say he knows what he's doing.

Next he proceeded to give instruction on how to cross-country ski. The first thing he told me was to stay in the tracks on the right. Pointing to the trail he said, "If you get off the tracks, you can trip up and hurt yourself. You can also get off into deep snow if you get out of the tracks. Someone has already prepared the trail for your convenience and safety."

So rule number one—stay in the tracks. Second rule—pace yourself. Get a rhythm going to insure a smooth stroke. He continued. Make sure you have water and snacks for energy. Be sure to head back in at five o'clock so you're back before dark. Have a great time and be safe! This guy could be trusted because of his knowledge and experience.

Well wouldn't you know, every time I got out of the track because I got scared or thought my way might be easier, I fell down. After four hours of enjoying the beautiful mountains, fresh air, and white snow, we were almost back when I took my ski out of the track to stop myself. My skis got crossways, and I tripped. I was so glad we were almost back since my ski snapped off and went flying down the hill onto an untouched valley of snow. Carrying my other ski, I walked back to the ski shop. I felt really bad going back with one ski, but I knew not to try and retrieve the other one because it was off the path.

We made it back before dark, I didn't hurt myself, and we had a blast! Feeling embarrassed, I explained to the ski instructor that I had lost a ski. He smiled and told us that only one other person in all these years had ever lost a ski. He was glad, however, that I hadn't tried to retrieve it myself because the snow in that area was very deep and lay over a pond. Whew!

Cherished

It's Easier Inside the Tracks

The purpose of the story: stay on track in your Christian walk. When you fall down, hold out your hand, and He will pick you up. When you choose to get off the track, the bruises, aches, and pains you endure will be lessons learned. Pick yourself up. Dust yourself off and hop back on the track.

I noticed something when I was on those tracks. When I got into a rhythm I became more confident and then I let myself glide. That was when I most enjoyed my surroundings, my friends, my God, and all that He had placed around me. I was in awe of my God! On the journey of life we really need to seek out the tracks God has already prepared for us. We can be confident that He's gone before us, that He's guarding our sides, and that He always has our back. We need to learn how to glide in our faith. Maybe you have heard the saying, "Let go and let God." Sounds good to me.

Where are you in your walk with God? Do you really love Him with your heart, your soul, and your mind? Do you trust Him with your life? Maybe you recognize after reading Matthew 22 that you have had the wrong focus. Maybe it's become more about tripping people up than finding "the answer." That sounds a lot like the Pharisees to me. It's unfortunate that we get so caught up in the religious or political aspects of faith that sometimes we can't see Jesus at all.

Join me in letting go and truly letting God move in your life. Experience His great love for you so that you will desire nothing greater than loving Him more. Pray and ask the Lord to help you stay on track, get back on track, or move you to a whole new set of tracks that He has made just for you to follow.

My Journal

Consider how great God's love is for you. Consider that He desires for you to love Him with your heart, mind, and soul. Close your eyes and picture Jesus telling you: "I love you so much I will never give up on you."

How does it make you feel knowing He longs for you to know Him and love Him that much?

~~~~~~

~~~~~~

~~~~~~

~~~~~~

~~~~~~

~~~~~~

~~~~~~

~~~~~~

~~~~~~

~~~~~~

~~~~~~

~~~~~~

~~~~~~

Cherished

Love Your Neighbor

"A second is equally important: 'Love your neighbor as yourself.'"
—Matthew 22:39

As a child, I loved to watch *Mister Rogers' Neighborhood*. This popular children's television show always started with a catchy song that reminds those watching to be neighborly. "It's a beautiful day in the neighborhood...Won't you be my neighbor?"

Funny how things we learn at a very young age stick with us for the rest of our lives. If you've ever seen or heard of this show you too know that everyone was Mr. Rogers's neighbor. He treated everyone with respect, kindness, and most of all, love. Let your mind zoom in on the neighborhood where you live. The houses, the apartment building, perhaps the community pool, the gas station, the grocery store, and most importantly, the people.

Write down some specifics that describe your neighborhood.

1. People
2. Houses
3. Gas Station
4. Dollar General
5. Restaurants

How many of your neighbors do you actually know by name? Can you list them?

1.

2.

3.

If you don't know their names, you may know them by description.

- ♥ The lady in the black SUV
- ♥ The kids who always leave their bikes in the yard
- ♥ The man with the beard
- ♥ The people who play loud music
- ♥ The girl who always makes out with her boyfriend in front of her house

Sad but true, we often form opinions of people by the way they look, smell, dress, or their form of transportation, clothing style, etc. And unfortunately, most of the time, our opinion is incorrect. What we don't see is the inside. We have no clue about their circumstances; we don't know what goes on behind the doors of their homes or more importantly, behind the doors of their hearts.

Stop for a moment and get a paper towel roll or toilet paper roll. When you look through the hole, be still and look at only one spot. Now look around the room without the roll. Can you see how that drastically changes your perspective? Many times this is how we look at people.

Read Matthew 10:5–9

"Go to the lost, confused people right here in the neighborhood" (The Message).

What a great reminder that we need to "go." Think about it. How often do you wait until your neighbor acknowledges you? As godly young

Cherished

ladies we need to be the ones who initiate the neighborly thing to do. Better yet, the godly thing to do. Could it be that we don't have time to speak, smile, or wave? Or perhaps the timing is simply not convenient? In fact, when God calls us to serve others, it's usually not convenient. Why? Because being a servant means you put the needs of others before your own.

Has there been a time recently when God prompted you to serve or be neighborly, but instead you rushed away from the opportunity?

Were you:

- ♥ Embarrassed?
- ♥ Too busy?
- ♥ Doing something for yourself?
- ♥ You really didn't want to go out of your way to make it work?

Write your thoughts.

Wow! That's powerful! To think that I rushed away from something because it wasn't convenient!

♥

In fact, when God calls us to serve others, it's usually not convenient. Why? Because being a servant means you put the needs of others before your own.

After living in San Antonio for 14 years we moved to Houston, Texas. The day we were moving in I said to myself, *"Chandra, you don't have friends here so you need to get to know your neighbors."* With that positive attitude, I did. For example, if they were outside when I drove up, I went over to introduce myself. As I would collect my mail I made sure to wave if they drove by. One of my neighbors was expecting a baby, so I kept watch and when the baby came, I took a gift over. Before I knew it I had several party invitations. I didn't really need any kitchen tools, jewelry, or clothing, but I accepted their invitations so I could meet my neighbors. Guess what? Now I know my neighbors. And of course, I ordered something at each one of those parties!

Someday you may have to move or change schools. Maybe you're moving now. Let me encourage you to take the initiative to meet new people. Or maybe you will be the neighbor who notices "the new girl" moving in. Go and meet her. That's what Jesus would want you to do. I'm not aware of any proper etiquette on who should say hello first. However, I do know that God commands us to love our neighbor. Listen to your heart and be obedient when the opportunity presents itself.

Tatenda's Story

I actually have a great story to share with you that proves when God's people love their neighbors the results can be life changing!

For years, youth camps have been one of my favorite places to hang out during the summer. While speaking at a camp one particular day my message was on God's provision. While preparing to speak, God continued to put "T" (a young man named Tatenda from the University of Mary Hardin-Baylor recreation team) on my heart. I didn't really know much about this young man other than every time he was around joy filled the area. He was radiant! His light was bright! His love for Jesus was contagious! It was evident students loved hanging out with T so I began to take notice. Right away it was clear that T treated everyone special. He noticed those who never got to go first or perhaps those who stood back because they weren't athletic. No problem for T. He knew just what they were good at. He never embarrassed anyone but somehow made everyone feel a part of the team. And his character, it drew students to him. This guy had the gift for loving people.

One morning at camp while preparing to share my message, I was praying at the back of the room. The Holy Spirit continued to put T's name and face before me. Quickly I found T and asked him if he would share his testimony when I called on him. He smiled the biggest, brightest smile and with his south African accent he graciously said, "Yes, Ms. Chandra! It would be my privilege to share." Little did I know that

Cherished

he had been praying: "Lord, use me this week, more than during the fun and games. Give me an opportunity to share my story with these students." I told you: God is so good!

Here's Tatenda's (T's) story in his own words:

♥ ♥ ♥

I grew up in Zimbabwe, a Third-World country in southern Africa. My mom is the head nurse at the biggest hospital in Zimbabwe, and my dad is a traveling preacher who graduated from the University of Mary Hardin-Baylor (UMHB) in Belton, Texas, and then from Dallas Theological Seminary. My dad was 36 when he started college, and at the time, international students received a considerable amount of scholarship money from the school. However, for me, UMHB represented the place where Daddy had graduated from, the place where he got lucky and was able to attend school, but it would never happen to anyone else in my family.

For as long as I could remember I worked at camps in Zimbabwe and truly believed that I would work my way up the camping system and eventually become camp manager. I was happy at the camp I worked at, had numerous friends, and it seemed as if the moment school was closed I was on the next bus to Sanganayi Creek, the camp where I truly loved working.

One day when I returned home from an end-of-year camp, my dad told me "Son, pack your bags; on Thursday you are leaving for UMHB." The day was Sunday, and in my mind, I was thinking that my dad wanted me to send a message to some of his former friends and then return home. I was so wrong. My dad was giving me five days notice that I was going to leave my comfort zone and go to a college where I did not know anyone in the area.

I was not thrilled about this plan but because my earthly father and heavenly Father had said so, I was going to step out in faith and believe God would take care of me. I thought I had grasped the concept of following Jesus when I became a Christian at age ten. But trusting in Jesus

I thought I had grasped the concept of following Jesus when I became a Christian at age ten. But trusting in Jesus is not as easy as it sounds.

is not as easy as it sounds. I was deeply saddened at the fact that I was not able to say good-bye to several of my close friends and was also not able to say farewell to my two grandmothers. My girlfriend of two and a half years saw it best to "dump me" at the airport, fearing that I would go to the United States and cheat on her. This was a huge blow to me because I honestly thought she was the one.

My dad gave me a $100 bill in case of emergency as I was about to board my plane. I had a number of connecting flights, and two of them were delayed, which meant I had to change flights. Eventually, my bags got lost in the airport system. This was my first time flying without my parents, and I was terrified to see this happen to me. This left me wondering why God had brought me to the States.

My bags took two weeks to be recovered, so basically I arrived in the land of the free and the home of the brave with a $100 bill and the clothes on my back. The international student director of UMHB told me to be positive and be excited about registering for classes the day after I arrived in the United States. So I got excited right up until the point the head cashier informed me that I owed $6,000 and wanted to know if I was going to pay with cash, check, debit, or credit card. I thought it was a big joke, because I only had $100 in my pocket and had never heard of all those other methods of payment.

A few moments later, the head cashier asked me if my plane ticket was a return ticket. They kept discussing ways they could get me back home, and I got scared. Here I was with no girlfriend, no money for college, no luggage, no clothes, no friends, and no family within 10,000 miles of me. I panicked and started sulking, saying "One day, I am going to be student body president of this school. One day, I am going to make good grades at this school. One day, I am going to have the possessions I need and help others."

God, through the kindness of His people, made my sulky, complaining, outlandish dreams come true. I got to my room and a $100 bill had been slipped under my door. Bear in mind I did not know anyone in the area, and so to find the bill was pretty mysterious. I went to have lunch and when I returned a huge bag of toiletries was sitting by my door.

Cherished

I got a phone call saying that one of my relatives had taken out a bunch of credit cards to help pay for my school. Every time I needed something God provided through His people, particularly my new church family, in a miraculous way. I am not an amazing, super-spiritual Christian; in fact, I am just a regular kid. However, it was amazing what happened to me through God and His people when I stepped out in faith. To take the cake, in the spring of 2007, I was elected the 92nd student body president of the University of Mary Hardin-Baylor and the first international student to be elected!

♥ ♥ ♥

Wow! God is so good! We saw God that day. Tatenda's story touched everyone in the room, and I pray it has touched you. God made a way. He answered T's prayer. He got to share his story. God's timing was perfect! T's story brings glory and honor to God. How wonderful to see how God's people reached out and made a difference in the life of their neighbor. When we become the hands and feet of Jesus, it's a beautiful thing!

Say these words of Jesus out loud: *"It is more blessed to give than to receive"* (Acts 20:35).

Has there been a time when someone reached out to you? Perhaps given you some needed money when you thought the situation seemed pretty hopeless?

What about a time when you had an opportunity to serve? Write down your memory. How did it change you? Was helping someone else a blessing for you?

♥
When we become the hands and feet of Jesus, it's a beautiful thing!

Love Your Neighbor?

What about that next-door neighbor or the one across the street? This week your task is to make a conscious effort to wave and say hello to your neighbors—a random act of kindness. If there are teenagers who live on your street or in your apartments, say hello to someone you usually don't acknowledge. Take your neighbor's newspaper or garbage can up to their door. Help someone who is elderly. Send a card. Smile at someone in the hallways at school. Pray that God will make you sensitive so when the opportunity to love your neighbor comes, you'll be ready and willing. The point is to become more aware of the people around you and then to be more Christlike in your actions.

Simply put, Galatians 5:13–14 tells us we are called to live in freedom, not to satisfy our sinful nature, but freedom to serve one another in love. For if the whole law can be summed up in five words, shouldn't we try to live accordingly? "Love your neighbor as yourself." Galatians 5:15 adds, *But if you are always biting and devouring one another, watch out! Beware of destroying each other.*

Would you agree that we are sometimes guilty of putting others down without realizing that our rude and hurtful words are really only about lifting ourselves up? This is exactly what Paul was teaching when he told us our freedom is not for building up our sinful nature. Think about it. When you share a negative comment about someone else or just have the nasty discussion about him or her within your own mind, what is the root of those mean thoughts?

OK, now that I've got you thinking, surely you are asking: So how do I fix this human flaw? You already accomplished the first thing; you recognize it. Admit it to God. Second, do something about it. Every time you have a selfish thought ask God to help you change it into something positive.

Remember: We cannot truly and fully love others until we love God. Loving God is the greatest command, and it is our minute-by-minute relationship with Him that enables us to fulfill the second command, loving our neighbors.

♥

Let's try this "love one another" thing. Try loving someone that perhaps you haven't.

74   Cherished

Unfortunately, the Lord just brought to my attention something I recently did. And of course, He would want me to give a personal example. Like I have already said, He's sure working on me.

While in my hair salon I noticed one of the stylists had totally changed her hair. I found myself thinking, *What in the world was she thinking? That style looks terrible on her...and the color! Her last hairstyle was so cute! Poor thing, she probably cries every time she looks in the mirror.* I caught myself having such critical thoughts. Then quickly the kinder side of me responded, *Or maybe she likes it, Chandra! Who are you to have such an opinion of her hairstyle?*

Then I thought about the many times I've had a bad hair day. After realizing what I had done I immediately changed my thoughts. *She's doing such a fabulous job on her client's hair and she seems so sweet.* It didn't take long before I had changed my negative thoughts into positive ones.

Reality is that we all have bigger problems than a bad hair day. Abuse, poverty, sickness, divorce, bad relationships, guilt, regret, secrets, bad grades, living up to someone else's expectations, etc. Let's try this "love one another" thing. Try loving someone that perhaps you haven't. Make a conscious effort to find something good in that person. If your thoughts are negative, change them to positive ones.

Or maybe you are having trouble letting go of the hurt someone has caused you. If this is you, forgive as Christ has forgiven you, so the Lord can begin to heal your hurts. As long as we hold on to those hurts, it keeps us from seeing God at work in us.

Satan loves it when we have hurt feelings, because they keep our focus on ourselves instead of others. This keeps Satan on the scoreboard of our lives. If he can keep us from loving God, loving others, and loving ourselves, he's the winner while we sit on the bench. Try and let the past stay in the past. Look ahead to the future. Today is a new day! God wants you on the playing field. In fact, you are one of His star players.

While I was ministering at a prison, an inmate shared this with me: behavior gets you into prison and behavior gets you out. Think about that for a minute. You get to choose your behavior. God-honoring choices always equal freedom. Jesus tells us to love our neighbor.

You get to choose your behavior. God-honoring choices always equal freedom. Jesus tells us to love our neighbor.

Random Acts of Kindness

While teaching a group of high school girls about "loving your neighbor" we decided to put action to our words. Everyone chose a beautiful flower from a bouquet in the middle of the room. At the end of our discussion we drove to a local fast-food restaurant where the girls were instructed to:

- ♥ Give the flowers away.
- ♥ Smile and be kind by reflecting the character of Jesus.
- ♥ Ask those dining how they are doing.
- ♥ Keep it real.
- ♥ Ask if you can pray for them.

♥

What can you do to serve others in your community? What's holding you back?

You should have seen the smiles in that place! Everyone wanted the girls to stay. Tears were shed when one of the girls held a hand across the table as she prayed a simple prayer with a complete stranger. One elderly lady shared how she eats alone every meal; it touched her so much that a young girl would care enough to sit with her while she ate. Another admitted being away from the Lord and shared how the prayer was just what was needed to get back on track.

The task was complete. The girls had made a difference. They felt good about what they had done and wanted to do it again. In fact they made a decision to get together once a month during that school year to start AOK, Acts of Kindness.

What can you do to serve others in your community? What's holding you back? Make a plan with your friends and go for it! If you can't meet with a group, you can do it on your own. Just this week I saw a teenage boy run up to a store entrance to hold the door open for a lady on crutches. What a great example of kindness.

Read Matthew 20:25–28.

You'll see how Jesus Himself came to serve, not to be served. Jesus is our greatest example of what it means to put others first and ourselves last. This teaching is the opposite of worldly values. Want to be a great leader? Start by serving others.

Serve

So whether you eat or drink or whatever you do, do it all for the glory of God....I don't just do what is best for me; I do what is best for others so that many may be saved.
—1 Corinthians 10:31–33

"Do to others as you would have them do to you."
—Luke 6:31 (NIV)

Encourage

Therefore encourage each other with these words.
—1 Thessalonians 4:18 (NIV)

Forgive

"If you forgive those who sin against you, your heavenly Father will forgive you."
—Matthew 6:14

Give

Each man should give what he has decided in his heart to give, not reluctantly or under compulsion, for God loves a cheerful giver.
—2 Corinthians 9:7 (NIV)

Show and Tell

When I served as a minister of youth, having a drama team was popular among many churches. Students would come up with creative skits, act out the lyrics of a song or use creative dance to interpret a message of truth with an audience. After our group was formed there were some important particulars the group needed to work on. The first thing we wanted to do was come up with a name for our group. We wanted the name to reflect our message. "Show and Tell" did just that. We would show people the character of Jesus in our skits and our telling was always intended to bring glory and honor to God.

Think about *show and tell* as a theme for your life. As Christians our life is a show-and-tell activity. People are always watching us. Neighbors, classmates, teachers, people at our job, our family, our best friends.

Who is watching you?

1.
2.
3.
4.
5.

Actually the number is likely much, much higher. We have no idea how many people are watching us. This week make a conscious effort to notice those around you. Then consider what they see, hear, and feel when they see you. Do they see a self-centered young lady who obviously only cares about herself or do they see a reflection of Jesus? Someone who is considerate, kind, and caring to those around her? Like my friend Tatenda, does your light shine bright? Or do you hide it under a bowl?

> *"You are the light of the world—like a city on a hilltop, that cannot be hidden. No one lights a lamp and then puts it under a basket. Instead a lamp is placed on a stand , where it gives light to everyone in the house. In the same way, let your good deeds shine out for all to see, so that everyone will praise your heavenly Father."*
> —Matthew 5:14–16

What a wonderful thing, to know your life is reflecting Christ to your neighbor. After all, this is your purpose in life. To glorify God so that others will come to know Him. It all goes back to "love your neighbor."

When It's Not Easy to Love Your Family

Why is it sometimes so hard to love those in your own family? Well, we love them because they are family, but sometimes we don't love to be with them because it's just no fun. It's more like torture. Can you relate? I hope this is common enough that you are saying to yourself right now: "I'm so glad she's going to touch on this!"

If anyone claims, "I am living in the light," but hates a Christian brother or sister, that person is still living in darkness. Anyone who loves another brother or sister is living in the light and does not cause others to stumble. But anyone who hates another brother or sister is still living and walking in darkness. Such a person doesn't know the way to go, having been blinded by the darkness.
—1 John 2:9–11

For many years, my brother Ronald and I had a strained relationship. I'll always remember one particular weekend, when our simmering tensions erupted. I said some things that were definitely unloving and could have caused him to stumble.

We were on a family camping trip. My parents, my brother and his family, my sister and her son, and, of course, Bruce, myself, and our two girls were all there. What we'd planned to be a wonderful family weekend ended rather quickly after Ronald and I got into a horrible fight.

Let me back up a little to give you some insight on our relationship. My brother and I (he's four years older) had not gotten along for years. We normally didn't fight; we just didn't speak. He had this way of intimidating everyone, especially me. It was common knowledge to family and friends that he didn't like me. He also thought that it was stupid (I can still hear him say those words) that I was so involved in church and that Bruce and I had Christian values that we actually lived by. He felt that I thought I was so much better than everyone else. After years of trying to be the nice sister, walking on eggshells at Christmases and other family gatherings, it happened! Like a steaming pot of water boiling on a stovetop I guess you could say the whistle finally blew! I'm sad to say now that it was ugly. He called me names and was very critical of me. I screamed back ugly things at him. Then I said some things that I regret to this day. Our family weekend was over before it had ever begun.

Years passed, and we saw each other at Christmas time, but it wasn't real enjoyable to say the least. Through the years we got the sad news that our daddy had colon cancer. After 16 months our dad passed away. Still…that awkward feeling, like the elephant in the room that everyone pretended wasn't there, *was there*.

For years I'd prayed, "Lord, what can I do? Lord, how can I serve You and love You and have such love for Your people yet have a brother who just might hate me?" Through the years there was always a dull pain in my heart. Being in youth ministry I was blessed to have a few godly men step into that brother role, but still I longed for my real brother to love me. I shared my hurt with close friends, and they too prayed for my brother and asked that someday God would restore our relationship. Ronald and I didn't see each other often, only when it was absolutely necessary. We would nod as each other entered a room and occasionally say hello.

One day when I was praying for my brother and his family, I know the Lord spoke to me, "Read my Word." I opened my Bible, and I knew I'd found what I'd been searching for all these years.

Dear friends, since God loved us that much, we surely ought to love each other. No one has ever seen God. But if we love each other, God lives in us, and his love is brought to full expression through us.
—1 John 4:11–12

That was it! Ronald would have to see God in me. I usually express my love to others in words, but it would have to be different with my brother. I would have to show him with my actions.

As I read this passage my eyes filled with tears. I could see the pain of Jesus on the Cross dying for my sin. Then clearly my heavenly Father said to my heart: "I did this for you because I love you. And I did this for your brother because I love him. Surely you ought to love each other."

"Lord, what can I do? Lord, how can I serve You and love You and have such love for Your people yet have a brother who just might hate me?"

Cherished

In that moment everything changed—my perspective, my heart. Finally I had a fresh desire to love my brother. I was ready, whatever it took. And then God gave me the opportunity to serve my brother. Not by words but by actions.

My brother is the daredevil of the family. His passion in life is going fast, jumping high, and entertaining large crowds! We got a call late one evening that Ronald had been in a serious motocross accident. Ronald had been racing in an arena when his glove somehow got caught on the throttle, a lever that causes the bike to speed up. While jumping from one hill to the next he instead went straight up in the air and quickly straight down. He landed on his feet, which jammed everything up like an accordion into his pelvis area. Both legs were badly broken; his pelvis and other body parts were in a mess. The doctors were saying he was very lucky not to be paralyzed. However, he would need to be off his feet for at least a year.

By the next morning, Ronald had come through emergency surgery in which the doctors had replaced many broken bones with pins and metal bars. He was in pretty bad shape.

"What do we do?" I asked Bruce.

"Well, you need to go," he replied.

Knowing my relationship with my brother was strained, my dear friend Leslie rode along with me to the hospital. We prayed for my brother, his wife and kids, and especially that I would have the right words to say to a brother with whom I hadn't had a real conversation in years.

I went into the intensive care unit. He had tubes coming out everywhere and was still on a breathing machine. He couldn't speak because of the tubes down his throat. I couldn't speak because my heart was in mine. Then my mouth opened and words begin to come out.

It's not important what I said that day, but when he tried to talk back he got choked on the tubes. Bells started ringing, nurses came running, and they made us leave the room. I couldn't believe it! What had I said that made him angry? I pretty much ran to the waiting room, got Leslie, and ran to the car. On the way home I cried as I went over and over what I had said and questioned how those few words could have upset him so badly. As we drove those three hours back home, my dear friend remarked that if I couldn't talk to my brother, then maybe this was the time I should minister to his family by talking to his wife. I thought about what she had said and it seemed right in my heart.

The next morning my mom called me. Knowing I had been upset, she too was hurting for both Ronald and me. Then she shared with me how as soon as they took the tubes out of Ronald's mouth that morning, the first thing he said was "I think I hurt Chandra's feelings." I started to cry.

My mom began to explain that he had been resting there unable to speak but had been thinking about exactly what I was telling him. He got choked trying to respond back to me. Thankfully, what I said had not made him angry. Isn't that just like Satan? Getting in the way of what God is doing. And this was going to be big!

Feeling much better, I called his wife Teresa. We talked more in those next six weeks than we had in ten years. She was able to cry with me and share things with me during those days that brought us closer than ever. The healing had begun; both in Ronald's physical body and within my heart. God was at work.

One day I felt that I had to call my brother. So I did. Ronald and I talked for 20 minutes. That was a miracle! Over the next weeks, while he was stuck in bed, we talked at least twice a week.

Bruce and I prayed and asked the Lord to show us how we could minister to my brother and his family. Ronald would be off work for close to a year. We were obedient, and we gave what God told us to give. They needed financial support, and God had made a way for us to help. Instead of words, God prompted us to give.

About eight weeks after the accident while on my way to an event the Holy Spirit tugged at my heart to call my brother, so I did. We talked for about 45 minutes. We laughed. We talked a little about our dad. We acted like brother and sister. We talked about his monster truck and motocross riding, things he enjoyed doing. Before the conversation was finished he even asked how my ministry was going. Amazing! To my surprise we have more in common than I ever thought. Not the racing part of course, but the people part. We both love being with people! Wait

Before the conversation was finished he even asked how my ministry was going. Amazing!

Cherished

a minute, that's not the best part of the story. On this day I witnessed another miracle. I ended the conversation by saying "I love you, Ronald, and I'm so glad you are getting better." And he said, "I love you too."

Miraculous!!! Do you still believe in miracles? I sure do!

My Prayer

Lord, thank You for loving me even when I'm not very lovable. Thank You for opening my eyes and heart to see others a little more like You do. Thank You that Your grace is sufficient for me. It is my desire to reflect You more and more each day of my life so I can become all You have created me to be. Beautiful, inside and out! A reflection of You! When I fail and begin to judge others or have unloving thoughts toward them, please, dear Lord, shake me, wake me, and remind me that You love them just like You love me. Because You love me, I should love my neighbor. Amen.

GAB Session
~ with Chandra ~

Changed for Good

"Why would I feel the need to serve someone who is mean to me?" Have you ever had that thought pass through your mind? We all have those hard-to-love people in our lives (and if they haven't shown up yet, believe me, they will).

But, through the written Word, we fall more and more in love with the Father. And this is the key that unlocks the door to our selfish desires and then fills us up with a passion to serve others. How wonderful that by drawing closer to the Father our "want-tos" change.

Read Matthew 5:43–48.

In this passage, Jesus teaches us to love our enemy. You know, it's easy to love people who love me back. It's easy to give to those who give to me. It's easy to hang out with my closest friends. But one of the greatest days of my life was the day I loved my hard-to-love brother, and he loved me back. God is so good!

Let me encourage you to love those who are hard to love. Maybe, as in my situation, there is someone in your family whom you feel treats you badly, who says hurtful things, or accuses you of things you know are not true. Pray for those people, but also pray that God will change your heart; pray, believing that God's love will shine through your actions in the midst of "hurt feelings." And yes, even love your enemy. Love them as Christ loves you. And one day maybe you too will witness a miracle!

"Then the King will say to those on his right, 'Come, you who are blessed by my Father; take your inheritance, the kingdom prepared for

Cherished

you since the creation of the world. For I was hungry and you gave me something to eat, I was thirsty and you gave me something to drink, I was a stranger and you invited me in, I needed clothes and you clothed me I was sick and you looked after me, I was in prison and you came to visit me.' Then the righteous will answer him, 'Lord, when did we see you hungry and feed you, or thirsty and give you something to drink? When did we see you a stranger and invite you in, or needing clothes and clothe you? When did we see you sick or in prison and go to visit you?' The King will reply, 'I tell you the truth, whatever you did for one of these brothers of mine, you did for me.'"
—Matthew 25:34–40 (NIV)

What a beautiful picture; that when we love one another we are showing others our love for the heavenly Father. Let me offer you a challenge. Keep this picture in your mind at all times, and the next time you have an opportunity to serve (love) someone in need, do it! I don't know about you, but this has changed my way of thinking. It gives me a "want to" attitude.

Read Philippians 2:3–4.

These verses clearly give testimony to my story. *"Don't be selfish"* (Philippians 2:3). I had to give the Lord my hurt feelings, so that I could be obedient and serve my brother. Unity through humility, God changed my heart. He humbled me by putting a desire in my heart to serve my brother, who had been my worst enemy. Can you see that when I took "myself" out of the picture, when I laid down my "hurt feelings," then it was easier to do what was right? All because of Jesus and His unfailing love for me—and my brother.

Take some time to read the Scriptures below. These give more direction when it comes to relationships.

♥ Worship: Psalm 15
♥ Revenge: Proverbs 24:29

♥ Judgment: James 2:12–13
♥ Truth: Ephesians 4:25–32

When Christ became the Lord and Savior of your life, there was a change, a metamorphosis.

Can you see the change in you? How have your attitudes toward other people changed?

Metamorphosis!

1 a: A change of physical form, structure, or substance especially by supernatural means **b:** a striking alteration in appearance, character, or circumstances
2 a typically marked and more or less abrupt developmental change in the form or structure of an animal (as a butterfly or a frog) occurring subsequent to birth or hatching

(Source: *Merriam-Webster's 11th Collegiate Dictionary*)

After reading this session is there a particular area where God is at work in you? How does He want to change you? Turn to the next page and take a few moments to write those thoughts down in your journal, along with any other important thoughts that have come to you during this study.

My Journal

Think about how God is changing you. In the space below, draw the most beautiful butterfly you can. Ask your heavenly Father to continue showing Himself to you so that you can continue to reflect Him.

session 4

Me, Love Myself?

"As yourself."
—Matthew 22:39

While ministering to young ladies around the country I have discovered that we don't know how to love ourselves, so we do a terrible job of loving others. The outcome? Well...it's ugly! The "mean girls" of pop culture are just a contemporary version of some of the bad girls you can read about in the Bible. For centuries, girls have struggled greatly with twisted views of themselves. While there are many reasons for this, I believe the primary reason is because they are not finding their foundation in a relationship with Jesus. Ignoring this great need, we girls spend a lot of time dwelling on negative thoughts about none other than ourselves. In other words: "Oh, poor me." Only through God's love can we love ourselves in a healthy way. He takes our focus off ourselves and directs it to Him and others. In the process, we lose the backbiting and backstabbing and develop a deep gratitude and appreciation for who we are in Him.

I know, I know...it's not about us. The Bible never teaches about "self-love." You're right! Our purpose is to glorify and love God. However, if we learn to see ourselves in light of Christ's love, the bondages of jealousy, pride, bitterness, self-hatred, and all that back

The Bible never teaches about "self-love." You're right! Our purpose is to glorify and love God.

biting and backstabbing go away. This leaves us free to love God more, love others, and shine for Jesus more than ever!

> Oh yes, you shaped me first inside, then out;
>> you formed me in my mother's womb.
> I thank you, High God—you're breathtaking!
>> Body and soul, I am marvelously made!
>> I worship in adoration—what a creation!
> You know me inside and out,
>> You know every bone in my body;
> You know exactly how I was made, bit by bit,
>> how I was sculpted from nothing into something.
> Like an open book, you watched me grow from conception
>>> to birth;
>> all the stages of my life were spread out before you,
> The days of my life all prepared
>> before I'd even lived one day.
> —Psalm 139:14–16 (*The Message*)

What beautiful words! What a perfect definition for one who is *cherished*! Can you see how much the Father loves you? Do you understand how beautiful you are? You are marvelously made! I believe the author of this psalm, under the direction of the Holy Spirit, assumes that you would and should love yourself. Not in a self-absorbed way, but rather because we are made in the image of God himself! We are so quick to let our circumstances define us instead of acknowledging who created us and loved us before we were born. This is the key message behind this study.

Why would God say to love Him with all our heart? Because your attitude is the aroma of your heart. If love for God is filling up your heart, then that's what will spill out. Think about it. Have you ever had something slip out of your mouth that you never intended? Of course you have. If it came out, guess what? It was there, in your heart. For out of the heart come desire, attitude, thoughts, actions, and words.

Cherished

♥

However, if we learn to see ourselves in light of Christ's love, the bondages of jealousy, pride, bitterness, self-hatred, and all that back biting and backstabbing go away. This leaves us free to love God more, love others, and shine for Jesus more than ever!

Explain aroma in your own words.

What has been the aroma of your heart lately?

When considering your heart, where do you struggle most?

- ♥ attitude
- ♥ desires
- ♥ thoughts
- ♥ actions
- ♥ words

Stop now and pray. In the psalm above, the words describe you as an "open book." Ask God, your heavenly Father, to help you take away the negative and selfish thoughts and turn them into good.

The Golden Rule

This might sound really strange, but would you want to be your friend? Well, we can't have this discussion until we look at the Golden Rule. Jesus tells us in Matthew 7:12 *"So in everything, do to others what you would have them do to you, for this sums up the Law and the Prophets"* (NIV). The phrase "the Law and the Prophets" refers to the commands God gave to Moses and others, which are written down in the Old Testament.

Note that Jesus begins this verse with "so" or "therefore." This is important. It ties everything in this verse to the context surrounding it. So, the Golden Rule depends on what was said right before.

Read Matthew 7:9–11.

Here's the context for the Golden Rule: it is based on our relationship to God as our Father who loves us and answers our prayers and gives good things to those who ask. In fact, this is the key to how we are able to love others as we love ourselves. God enables us to keep the Golden Rule by

His fatherly provision. His love for us and our trusting response of love back to him is the source of power for loving others. It is also the source for how we can really accept and love ourselves.

Stop here for just a moment. Earnestly ask the Lord to open your heart to truth, so you can answer these questions honestly. Ask Him to shine light on those areas that have over time become darkened by selfish pride. These may include attitudes and thoughts that need adjusting. The questions below will help you become more aware of how you act and how others perceive you. Please don't think of this as a contest if you are sharing your answers with a group of girls. This is between you and God. Be honest with yourself. Allow God to strip away pride, so He can begin to change you, repair you, and restore you. Although this task might not be so fun, it will be good for you in the end.

Take a moment and ask yourself these questions. Hold a mirror up to your inner self.

Am I a good friend?

How do others see me?

What do I really think about myself?

Do I love others? Give a reason for your answer.

Do I love myself? Why or why not?

Cherished

Who and what do I reflect?

How do I speak to others?

How do I speak about others?

In general, how do I treat others?

Do I reflect the world? ME ME ME? Or do I reflect my heavenly Father?

Polished and Shiny!

Noticing my rings were looking murky and dull, I dropped them off at the jewelry store so they could be professionally cleaned. The rings included my wedding rings and a blue topaz ring that I had not worn in a while because I just didn't really like it anymore. After running a few errands I stopped to pick up the rings. *Wow!* I couldn't believe how beautiful and shiny they looked. The brilliant color glistened from the diamonds on my wedding band. And the clear blue topaz, well, I was amazed! It seemed as though I had just picked up new rings! I called and thanked Bruce all over again! They were beautiful! I immediately put them on and stared at them all the way home and often throughout the next few days.

When I took the rings to be cleaned it felt like a chore: "I have to take these rings in and get them cleaned…bah humbug." But my attitude sure changed when I saw them cleaned and restored to the way they first looked. I have to admit I had forgotten how beautiful they were, yet I had them on all along.

Similar principles can apply to our life with Christ. We don't take care of our self. Well, maybe we take care of the outer appearance, hoping and thinking that looking good will make us *feel* better. But, the inside, the spiritual body, the heart—you know, the part that really matters? Too often we neglect it, allowing it to become murky and dull! We get stuck in a rut, busy living out our everyday routine. The joy of our salvation has faded over time. We quickly forget what Jesus Christ has done for us. Instead, we take charge and live our life our way. Once we were joyfully shining for Jesus, reading our new Bible, flipping through the pages like a treasure map. Now we give little or no attention to caring for the inside, the foundation where our life either blooms or dries up. But then one day "something" happens that brings Christ back to the forefront of our heart, our mind, and we take time to get out of the rut and meet with Him again. Just like the diamonds, He polishes us up when we spend time with Him. Oh yes, that "something" that happens—it's God pursuing you, the one He cherishes.

Funny how I can see my daddy polishing his shoes, moving the polishing rag back and forth with quick strokes. He was shining them up for church, wanting to look his best while entering into worship. I can see Jesus, as I sit and talk with him, polishing me up to prepare my heart for worship.

No Pedestals Here

Some girls love themselves in a "self-love" kind of way. Many of these girls are narcissistic and spoiled, and everything is all about them. These girls are desperate for words of affirmation. Receiving a compliment or being better (in their eyes) than everyone around them is empowering. They are about building themselves up. Get the picture? In other words, it's all about me, myself, and I!

Having a servant's heart is far from these girls' minds unless they are after brownie points with a certain group, seeking acceptance, or trying to impress adults who see the "good deed." Their hearts are not right. They do everything for applause. They can be conceited, judgmental, and their thoughts may go something like this, *"I look sooo much better than her."* Or, *"I'm sooo much better than them."* They only reflect

♥

I can see Jesus, as I sit and talk with him, polishing me up to prepare my heart for worship.

Cherished

themselves, certainly not Christ. The really sad thing is that they are so caught up in their own tiny worlds that they don't recognize their downward spiral. If you pour yourself back into self you will never get anywhere or anything but *selfish*!

Now, hear me correctly on this one. As godly and beautiful girls there is nothing inherently wrong with wanting to look our best—well cared for hair, nice makeup, cute clothing—the difference though is found in the heart.

Usually, there is something deeper going on in these girls who are *so* into themselves. Perhaps they don't feel loved by their parents. Maybe they don't get enough nurturing from their moms. Or maybe they have been hurt in the past, and Satan continues to use guilt, anger, hurt feelings, or a particular sin to destroy them. They seek attention to cover the hurt and fill themselves up with a false, misdirected sense of love. Again, this will never be enough. They're caught in a trap, like a mouse running in a spinning wheel with no escape.

> If this describes you, don't let Satan keep you in bondage. Freedom awaits you if you call on the name of Jesus. Get off the spinning wheel now!

It's not pretty, is it? You may know one of these girls. You may be one of these girls. There are many young ladies and even women who have a compulsive need to be recognized. Do you know that never in God's Word does He tell us we should be put on a pedestal? No! Quite the contrary; take a look in your Bible at Paul's great example for this discussion: 1 Corinthians 10:31–33.

- ♥ Whatever you do, do it all for the glory of God.
- ♥ Don't cause anyone to stumble.
- ♥ Don't seek your own good, but the good of many.
- ♥ Ultimately follow the example of Christ.

It is always better to put others before yourself, as this will develop more Christlike characteristics and a servant's attitude. Sorry girls, no mention of pedestal here.

Read Matthew 19:16–30.

Jesus is speaking to a rich young man. Once again, in verse 19, we see the importance of the commandment: love your neighbor as yourself.

In verses 23 and 24, Jesus talks about entering the kingdom of God. Everyone knows it is impossible for a camel to fit through the eye of a needle. That's exactly his point. Then the disciples basically ask, "So who can be saved?" Don't you love how Jesus doesn't leave us guessing when He answers their question? *"Humanly speaking, it is impossible. But with God everything is possible"* (Matthew 19:26). The greater teaching here is that with Christ all things are possible; He's the one who saves us. It's not about being rich or poor as to who gains entrance to heaven.

And my favorite teaching on this whole pedestal idea is found in verse 30. Jesus says many who are first will be last and many who are last will be first. If I were a fly on the wall of your brain I can just hear it now. *"Oh no! That messes up everything! The world's concept is just the opposite."* You've got that right! Are you willing to trust God in this, which may mean that you come in last today and a lot of other days too? Can you see where the gain is? We benefit by choosing God's approval over the approval of others? Wow! This is something to ponder.

Take a moment and think back over the last two weeks. Have there been times you opted for first when now you can see how last would have brought a smile to God's face and put a joyful skip in your heart?

Putting Others First

Bruce and I were in Chicago recently spending a special few days together. One night we dressed up and enjoyed a nice dinner. Too full for dessert, we ordered it to go. Afterwards we took in views of the Chicago skyline from the sky deck of the Sears Tower, one of the world's tallest buildings. It was a thrilling night!

While walking back to our hotel, discussing what a blessing it was to have this treasured time together, we noticed a homeless man and a little boy, who was maybe four years old. The man asked us if we could help him out. Without hesitation Bruce gave him the bag with the dessert in it. The little boy's face—oh my goodness!—it lit up like someone who had just won a million dollars. Although I had been dreaming of that dark chocolate forest cake, it was so much more satisfying to give it away. I only wish I had some cold milk to give them too.

It was only a very small thing we gave, but it taught me a lot. I don't share this story to boast in our action; I'm boasting only in our God. The willingness to give away something we'd bought for ourselves came from God's love, which lives inside of us. This story is an example to how opportunity comes when you least expect it. It is also a good example of how putting someone first can be such a blessing. This Christlike standard for living can apply to many areas of our daily life.

It's obvious to me that the rich and famous, and even sometimes those who hold high leadership positions in companies and churches, have many hardships. We lift them up and put them on a pedestal. The pedestal starts to crumble over time and they fall down. Some of these famous people feel they are indestructible. Nothing can hurt them. They can afford to buy anything, even buy themselves out of much-earned consequences. But someday, they will self-destruct. And unfortunately they will crash, bringing those closest to them down with them. We've seen it in the news. Can you think of a few people in the spotlight who have fallen off the pedestal?

Ladies, put the pedestal positioning out of your mind. You don't want to be there anyway.

Read Matthew 19:28–30 again.

Ladies, put the pedestal positioning out of your mind. You don't want to be there anyway. It screams "me first!" It's a turnoff for most people; it's also the last place we should want or desire to be as servants of Jesus Christ. He should always be the only One upheld, the One worthy of praise and applause. He sits on the only pedestal that matters. He sits on the throne!

Perhaps you have been the girl who longed for the applause of others. If we're honest, we've all been caught up in a me-first world many times. Isn't it tiring? Always trying to put on a show, wear the right mask, wanting desperately to have the applause of others.

Read 1 Corinthians 13:4–7.

What a great reminder of what love is and what it is not. Does your heart feel a bit heavy right now? How many times have you been rude to someone lately? Maybe you have kept a record of someone who has hurt you in the past. Or maybe you kept something for yourself, as simple as a piece of cake, knowing someone close by needed it more than you.

Read 1 Peter 3:3–5.

What is God speaking to you through His Words? What are your thoughts? Journal them below.

Erica's Story

Erica (not her real name) felt she was never good enough for her parents. Her family was very competitive. She, however, didn't enjoy being on the basketball team, the math team, or any team for that matter. She was fine making good grades in school and having only a few close friends. After graduating college with a 4.0, her parents pushed her to continue her education in law school.

"Be something great!" her dad said. He knew that Erica had the desire to work with the preschool children at her church, but he told her she was too smart for that and would never make any money working at the church. If she heard it once she had heard it a thousand times.

"I'd rather be happy than wealthy," she said, "and working with children will make me happy, Dad. It's what I believe God has purposed me to do." Her dad shook his head with disappointment and left the room.

It had been years and still his hurtful words—"You're smarter than that"— ran through her mind like sand in an hourglass. Like most daughters she wanted to please her dad, to make him proud. She thought if she became a really successful preschool director he would someday understand and be proud of her.

Needless to say, she didn't go to law school. She did, however, become a children's minister. She began spending hours studying the Bible, memorizing hundreds of chapters of both the Old and New Testaments as if to prove her intelligence. She had become somewhat of a biblical scholar. Her dad and others were impressed with her wealth of knowledge. She had read the Bible many times over and was quick to let you know just how many times. What she couldn't see was that Satan was using something good as a vise that begin to grip her heart more and more tightly. He wanted to use her weakness (the desire to prove herself to her dad) to destroy her, to steal her joy. Always trying to prove she knew more than the next person, her study became obsessive.

Oddly enough, having knowledge and memorizing Scripture became an addiction to her, like a person who exercises constantly or doesn't eat, in order to lose weight. Satan exploited her pride and her desire to prove herself. Unaware, she had allowed words from her past to become a stronghold in her life.

Erica had become prideful and self-righteous; like weeds in a garden, her ugly attitudes had taken over her heart. Correcting others, even people on church staff, was fun to her. It built her up and she liked the feeling of "winning." Her knowledge became intimidating to those who worked with her. It wasn't long before her unloving attitude caused church members to stay away from the preschool area; some who had been hurt even left the church. This had become a real problem, and the church had no other choice but to confront her in a special meeting. It was during this meeting the dam that had held all that hurt in for so many years finally broke. Her tears flowed like a river. She cried out, "I was never good enough! Not to my dad, not to you, not to anyone!"

She realized those hurtful words from her father had taken root in her heart. Over time they became briars that choked out new life and joy. Her heart had become hard. She was living in bondage. The tears that had been stored up for years finally flowed freely. On that day Erica gave up on "self." She gave up trying to be good enough. Instead, she chose to bask in the love of her heavenly Father, and finally she was set free.

Everything changed that day. She shared her story. She shared that through Jesus God had forgiven her and asked that they would also forgive her. There were many happy and joyful tears shed that day. With Erica's changed heart, the preschool ministry began to thrive. Because the weeds and briars had been pulled from her heart by the Master Gardener (John 15) she began living life in full bloom.

Read John 10:10.

Satan is real. He is sly! He uses our hurts and fears to affect our relationship with God. Obviously these strongholds put distance between us and God. Perhaps we begin to feel unworthy of His love. Or we may begin to wonder if God is even real.

♥

As believers, we must grow up. Learn to turn the other cheek. Be willing to forgive and forget.

Cherished

When my girls were little, they had biters in their preschool class. You know—kids that bite. One child would bite so the one who had been bitten would instinctively bite back. Before the teacher knew it, everyone was crying.

Unfortunately, it's kind of the same with young ladies and women. (See Galatians 5:15.) We get hurt, so we too are quick to bite back. As believers, we must grow up. Learn to turn the other cheek. Be willing to forgive and forget. Ouch! That's tough! This, my sister, is spiritual maturity. When we read the Bible and begin to understand grace and mercy only then will we become more like Jesus. Only then will we be able to love our neighbor as ourself.

> *Above all else, guard your heart, for it is the wellspring of life.*
> —Proverbs 4:23 (NIV)

What does this verse mean by "the wellspring of life"?

Do you recognize strongholds in your heart? If so, can you see how Satan is holding you captive by those things?

Do you remember what you should say? "He who is in me is greater than he who is in the world" (paraphrase from 1 John 4:4).

Talk with Jesus and keep that open-book mentality. By knowing His love is flowing through us, we can have self-control in these hurtful situations. In fact, God's love working in us will give us the desire to love our neighbor.

God Loves You

How do you love yourself? Forget about yourself. Yep! Strange but true. Properly understood, that's what the Bible tells us. Listen to this:

"What's the price of a pet canary? Some loose change, right? And God cares what happens to it even more than you do. He pays even greater attention to you, down to the last detail—even numbering the hairs on your head! So don't be intimidated by all this bully talk. You're worth more than a million canaries. Stand up for me against world opinion and I'll stand up for you before my Father in heaven. If you turn tail and run, do you think I'll cover for you?

If you don't go all the way with me, through thick and thin, you don't deserve me. If your first concern is to look after yourself, you'll never find yourself. But if you forget about yourself and look to me, you'll find both yourself and me."
—Matthew 10:29–33, 38–39 (*The Message*)

The Father loves you! He is jealous for you. He wants you to love Him more than anything else or anyone else. Do you see that? We so often look to find ourselves, but do you see the picture He has painted before us? God, your Father, loves you more than you can imagine. He knows everything about you, even how many hairs are on your head. He has placed so much value on you. Nothing can take away God's love from you. Nothing! There will be times when family members and dear friends disagree with God's truth. He is asking you to stand up for Him and His truth. We must pick up our cross. What does this mean exactly? We must go public with our love for Jesus Christ. We will face opposition. All that seems so grand and important here in this life will leave us feeling empty in the end. Money, power, popularity, trophies, "stuff," prestige, fame—it's all nothing when compared to eternal life and all that we will inherit. Remember, this life is temporary. Eternal life with Jesus in heaven is forever! Wow! This always gets me so excited!

So, do you see why Jesus tells us to love Him with everything that we are and everything that we have? In the end, He is all that matters. When we love Him we have the answer to living this life on earth with hope and joy no matter what our circumstance.

Cherished

With all my faults and flaws I've chosen to surrender my life to Jesus, and I don't want to live any other way. Without Jesus Christ in my life I am *nothing*!

Read John 3:16.

If you still have trouble loving yourself after hearing how much God your Father and Creator loves you, adores you, cherishes you, I'm determined for you to love yourself by the time this session is over.

♥ Be thankful!

♥ Remember, you are created in God's own image. Wow!

♥ God put you over the fish of the sea, the birds of the air, over the cattle, and over all the earth, and over every creeping thing that creepeth upon the earth! (See Genesis 1:25).

Your Body

In this section, I'd like to stop and address an issue that most young women struggle with—their bodies. Are you like every other girl or woman who doesn't like something about her body? We can be so critical of ourselves, can't we?

Today I was working out at the gym and the only other person in the room was a physically fit, middle-aged woman. She was running on the treadmill when I got there and was still running when I left. Of course, she was in very good shape. You could tell by looking at her seemingly perfectly chiseled body. Not that I was staring or anything. As I walked briskly on the treadmill for 45 minutes, I began to get down on myself, so I quickly changed those negative thoughts to positive ones.

After writing this study I can truly say, "Thank You, God, for making me just the way that I am." My talk with the heavenly Father sounded something like this.

"Lord, I am marvelously made and I desire to take good care of this body You gave me. I get that You didn't make me a runner or a great athlete. But, God, You did give me my daddy's pretty eyes and love for people. You put a scoop of cheer in me, so that I can cheer the runner on. Your marvelous work gave me legs so I can walk, arms so I can hug, and a head with a brain so that I can think, remember, and make decisions. You gave me strong bones and veins that keep the blood flowing, that keep my heart pounding, which keeps me alive! Lord, You made me a woman so I could have the joy of giving birth and being a mom to two beautiful girls. You gave me lips so I could kiss my husband, Bruce. Lord, You pursue me and continue to draw me close. Lord, thank You for loving me with all my flaws and imperfections. Thank You that through life's ups and downs I have come to understand that You tenderly care for me, love me, adore me, give me a desire to do your will, and Lord, so much more. Thank You, Father, for Your written Word that helps me know You more intimately. Lord, thank You for making me 'me.' I love You, Father."

Take a few minutes to recognize all that you can do because of the body God created for you. Then share your heart with God.

Thank You God for making me.

Christ in Us

Can you see now that what you think about you makes a difference in how you love your neighbor as yourself? As daughters of the King we must change our way of thinking. Think about this.

I have been crucified with Christ and I no longer live, but Christ lives in me. The life I live in the body, I live by faith in the Son of God, who loved me and gave himself for me.
—Galatians 2:20 (NIV)

If we are to love Christ and if Christ lives in us and we are one when we are united with Him, then it makes sense that we would love ourselves. And it's easy to see this love has nothing to do with a narcissistic (self-centered) kind of love. It is Christ within us that helps us die to "self" each day. Colossians 1:27 reads, *God has chosen to make known among the Gentiles the glorious riches of this mystery, which is Christ in you, the hope of glory"* (NIV).

Once you understand that you are one with Christ Jesus and that the Holy Spirit you received at the time of salvation is very real, you will begin to experience joy, thankfulness, love, guidance, and forgiveness like never before. You will also graciously know that it comes from nothing you have done but everything He has done through you.

My Prayer

Lord, I praise You for making me special! I praise You for giving me the gift of the Holy Spirit, who gives me the strength to make it through challenging times. When I am hurt by what others say or when I think thoughts about myself that hurt or put me down, may Your power in me quickly take captive those negative thoughts. Prevent them from taking root in my mind and in my heart. Lord, I pray after reading this session and studying Your Word that these truths would penetrate deep within my heart to remind me how valuable I am to You! Lord, my desire is to know You more, so that I will love You more and more and more each day. I am confident in Your promises, and I believe that You love me and that You think I am beautiful just the way that I am. Lord, I pray that my heart would begin to look more like Yours so that when I look in the mirror I can walk with confidence knowing that I am a reflection of my Father. Then I will finally see how I should love myself. Amen.

GAB Session
~ with Chandra ~

Tootsie and the Toad

On a Monday morning while snuggled in my soft, warm, oh-so-cozy bed, I was awakened by cries of "Moooom!" I continued to lie in my bed hoping the call was just a dream. Bruce was home and we were planning to sleep in until eight.

"Moooom!! Tootsie's chasing a frog and I think she's eating it!"

The loud call was coming from our oldest daughter, Lindsey, who was in the kitchen. She and her puppy Tootsie were home for the summer.

By the third call, Lindsey was actually starting to cry. Of course she knew that if she cried I would come, despite the fact it was only 5:30 in the morning!

"OK," I said to Bruce as he rolled over, "I guess I better get up and see what in the world is going on!" I'm not a morning person, so I wasn't too happy.

Right away I could see that Tootsie had a frog (actually a toad) cornered, and I was sure by this time all our neighbors were also awake on this early summer morning. The good news was Tootsie wasn't eating the toad. The bad news was she had slime bubbling out of her mouth. When seized, toads secrete a nasty slime to defend themselves. This slime works almost like mace. It tastes awful and can burn the eyes of its victim.

Now the reason I want to share this story with you is because of what Tootsie did next. I picked Tootsie up, and we gave her a quick bath in the sink. Her right eye was swollen shut, so I also squeezed water in it to help rinse out the slime. The poor dog looked like she had been in a fistfight. She was snorting and swaying from side to side as she walked,

Cherished

but the second that we put her down, you guessed it…she went right back to the frog. The one who had caused her all this harm was beckoning her back.

My sister, my friend, beloved child of God, cherished daughter, stop going back to those things that hurt you the most. If it's a thought, replace that hurtful thought with something good. If it's a friend, she's no friend at all. If it's a boy, run away from immorality. If it's someone who hurts you, tell someone you trust. If it's guilt, you've been forgiven. If it's secrets, expose them and seek truth. If it's lack of confidence, continue to seek His Word. If it's anxiety, seek the Lord and see a doctor and/or counselor. Run to Jesus; let Him dust you off, polish you up, and make you shine like new again.

How to Love Yourself
...Because He First Loved You

I've written this guide to help you see yourself in the light of God's love for you.

♥ *Stop all hurtful criticism.* Criticism alone never changes a thing. Refuse to beat yourself up. If you need to make some changes, do it! Everybody changes. When you cut yourself down, your changes are negative. When you approve of yourself, your changes are positive. Be good to yourself!

♥ *Don't scare yourself.* Stop scaring yourself with bad thoughts. It's a dreadful way to live. Self-hatred is hating your own thoughts. Change your thoughts. Philippians 4:8 says: *"Fix your thoughts on what is true, and honorable, and right, and pure, and lovely, and admirable. Think about things that are excellent and worthy of praise."* Negative and hurtful thoughts are not from the Lord.

♥ *Be kind to yourself.* Galatians 5:22–23 says: *"But the fruit of the Spirit is love, joy, peace, patience, kindness, goodness, faithfulness, gentleness, and self-control. Against such things there is no law"* (NIV). Your thoughts, even toward yourself, should reflect these qualities of the Spirit.

♥ *Live in freedom.* Paul writes in Galatians 5:1: *"It is for freedom that Christ has set us free. Stand firm, then, and do not let yourselves be burdened again by a yoke of slavery"* (NIV). When facing trials and troubles, when you feel defeated, say out loud, "I am free in Christ!" Don't allow Satan to have a stronghold in your life. The devil knows your weakness, but remember, when you're weak God is strong.

- ♥ *Try a little praise.* Criticism breaks your inner spirit. Praise builds it up. Praise the Lord and thank Him for who you are because He is in you! Sometimes, we simply have to be good to ourselves with kind words or a self-pat on the back. It's OK!

- ♥ *Support yourself.* Find ways to support yourself. Reach out to friends, your parents or youth pastors, and doctors; allow them to help you. Be strong; don't be shy to ask for help when you need it.

- ♥ *Be loving to others.* When you do something nice for your parents, your friends, your teachers, your siblings, or anyone at all, it's not just good for them, it's good for you too. Love one another. Remember, you reap what you sow.

- ♥ *Take care of your body.* Learn about nutrition. What kind of fuel does your body need to have energy and vitality? Learn about exercise and discover what you enjoy. You can choose to be clean. You can choose to be neat. Ultimately you choose how you look. Remember, it's the inner you that people enjoy being around. Keep this in mind: when you are planted on the firm foundation of Jesus Christ, you can't help but grow into a beautiful young woman. Your smile, your fragrance, your joy will draw others to you.

- ♥ *Mirror work.* Look into your own eyes often. Express a growing sense of gratefulness for what God is doing in you. Forgive yourself when needed and go on. Talk to people in the mirror whom you need to forgive. Talk to the Lord in the mirror. Thank Him for making you "you." Pray that you will be a reflection of Him to those who look at you. Remember, self-centered love is not from God.

- ♥ *Love yourself—do it now!* Don't wait until you look your best, lose the weight, get the braces off, don't have pimples, don't have bad hair. Instead, thank God for making you special, unique, and beautiful! *"I praise you because I am fearfully and wonderfully made; your works are wonderful"* (Psalm 139:14 NIV).

My Journal

Think back to the beginning of this session. What was your first thought when you read the title: "Me, Love Myself?" Write down your thoughts. How are you different now than when you first began this study?

~~~~~~

~~~~~~

~~~~~~

~~~~~~

~~~~~~

~~~~~~

~~~~~~

~~~~~~

~~~~~~

~~~~~~

~~~~~~

~~~~~~

~~~~~~

~~~~~~

Cherished

Passion To Serve

"You are the light of the world—like a city on a hilltop that cannot be hidden. No one lights a lamp and then puts it under a basket. Instead, a lamp is placed on a stand, where it gives light to everyone in the house. In the same way, let your good deeds shine out for all to see, so that everyone will praise your heavenly Father."
—Matthew 5:14–16

Christians are called to shine! We shine when we reflect Jesus. We shine when we love others. We shine when we share the gospel! *"Shine like stars in the universe as you hold out the word of life"* (Philippians 2:15–16 NIV). Just as Jesus Christ came to seek and save the lost, so we too should go into all the world and share this good news. Some serve in their community through their jobs or in their school; all Christians are called to that "wherever" place God has sent them. There are so many places in the world where God wants to put His people. It could be down the street, in your classroom, in your home, or around the world. John 3:16 tells us that God loves the whole world. Therefore we too should love the whole world.

Read Matthew 28:18–20.

Jesus told his disciples this just before He ascended to heaven:

> *"But you will receive power when the Holy Spirit has come upon you. And you will be my witnesses, telling people about me everywhere—in Jerusalem, throughout Judea, in Samaria, and to the ends of the earth."*
> —Acts 1:8

Growing up in a Baptist church I was taught about missions. Girls in Action® and Acteens® are missions organizations for girls first through twelfth grade. While many of my friends were involved in Brownies and Girls Scouts I went to the Wednesday night missions study at church. It was fun! We served in our Jerusalem, which means our local community. Visiting nursing homes and shut-ins (elderly people who cannot go out of their homes), taking sandwiches to the homeless, singing and doing silly skits, slumber parties, making Christmas cards for prisoners—every one of these events was about sharing the love and hope of Jesus Christ!

Now I don't want to sound like I was this perfect girl who wouldn't miss Wednesday nights for anything. Believe me, there were times in middle school and high school when my friends and I would get so bored as the missionaries showed their slides and shared their testimonies for what seemed like hours. We would talk and giggle and get in all kinds of trouble. And I know my mother and I went round and round more than once on why I had to go to church on Wednesday nights. But now here I am writing a whole session about missions.

One of the most significant things we did on those Wednesday nights was praying for missionaries by name on their birthday. And we learned about those who had given their lives to spread the gospel and care for the needy. Lottie Moon and Annie Armstrong are two missionaries I especially remember learning about because of the great heritage they left for us. Even then I was drawn to the work of Lottie Moon; God used this little lady (she was only four foot three) in a mighty way. In the late 1800s and early 1900s, during Lottie's lifetime, it was uncommon for an unmarried woman to serve on the missions field. Lottie overcame those who criticized her and instead kept her focus on the passion and vision God

♥

Little did I know the impact praying for missionaries would have on my life.

Cherished

had given her to reach people in China for Christ. Little did I know the impact praying for missionaries would have on my life. The foundation was being laid as early as I can remember; God was preparing me then for what my passion is today: sharing the good news of Jesus with people all over the world. I hope my testimony can be encouraging to you!

I'd like to share a little more of Lottie Moon's story with you. She was an amazing lady, obviously long before my time. However, her story captivated me and gave me a personal interest for missions. Now I'll pass her story along to you in hopes that if God has already begun to put these missional desires in your heart you will be inspired to press on.

♥ ♥ ♥

Lottie's Story

Charlotte Digges "Lottie" Moon was born in December 1840 to Anna Maria and Edward Harris Moon on their Viewmont estate in Virginia. Her parents were devout Christians, and she was saved at age 18.

Out of obedience to God's call on her life, she sailed to China as a missionary in 1873. As an unmarried woman, she faced particular challenges both in the Chinese culture and, at times, from her fellow missionaries and folks back home. Throughout her life, she remained adamant that more missionaries were needed for China, including female missionaries. She persevered through personal loneliness and deprivation to become a powerful advocate, particularly through her letters, for missions in China, and, ultimately, the whole world. Over nearly 40 years, she gave herself unceasingly to the cause of Christ, primarily sharing God's love with the beloved Chinese women, children, and men she served until her death.

"To the Chinese, she became a lady teacher who would talk books, a wonderful cookie maker, a critic of foot binding, and, in the end, a fellow sufferer," writes Cathy Butler in the *The Story of Lottie Moon*. The early 1900s were a time of persecution, violence, and upheaval in China as the last dynasty fell to pieces. Lottie suffered along with her Chinese brothers and sisters, and by 1912 she had become extremely weak and ill. In an effort to save her, fellow missionaries urged her to return to America for recovery. She died en route, on board a ship in Japan.

Her legacy in China is great, but perhaps her most significant contribution to missions was her encouragement of the support of missionaries by prayer, finances, and other means. In 1888, a handful of US women dedicated to the cause of worldwide missions, led by Annie Armstrong and inspired by the urgent pleadings of Lottie Moon's letters, founded Woman's Missionary Union®. That year at Christmas they raised about $3,300 for the support of new missionaries. In 1918, at Annie Armstrong's suggestion, the annual WMU offering became the Lottie Moon Christmas Offering® and has been collected every year since by local churches for the Southern Baptist International Mission Board (IMB). In 2007, just over $150 million was collected through this offering, every penny of which goes to support the more than 5,000 IMB missionaries sharing the gospel overseas. WMU has today become the largest Protestant organization for women in the world, with a membership of approximately 1 million.

(Source consulted: *The Story of Lottie Moon* by Cathy Butler. For more information on Annie Armstrong, see *The Story of Annie Armstrong* by Cathy Butler. These books are available through www.WMUstore.com.)

♥ ♥ ♥

The Heartbeat of God

> *"Love the Lord your God with all your heart and with all your soul and all your mind.' This is the first and greatest commandment. And the second is like it: 'Love your neighbor as yourself.'"*
> —Matthew 22:39 (NIV)

From the very beginning of this study we have talked about the importance of these two great commandments. It just makes sense that we would talk about serving others.

Did you know God is searching for those who are willing and ready to serve Him?

For the eyes of the LORD range throughout the earth to strengthen those whose hearts are fully committed to him.
—2 Chronicles 16:9 (NIV)

Let me try and explain this verse in my own words. When you have a close relationship with Jesus, you begin to get a glimpse of the heartbeat of God. It's supernatural! It's hard to explain it. The Holy Spirit begins to show you new things, to change your perspective, and to grow you up in spiritual things. God is looking throughout the whole world to show Himself to those who desire, hunger, and crave to know Him more.

Crave...it's a strong word, don't you agree? When you are at this place in your relationship with God anything can happen! Once you get a taste of how sweet God's goodness is, you'll long for more.

No eye has seen, no ear has heard, and no mind has imagined what God has prepared for those who love him. But it was to us that God has revealed these things to us by his Spirit. For his Spirit searches out everything and shows us even God's deep secrets.
—1 Corinthians 2:9–10

Wow! I don't know about you but count me in! Who wouldn't desire to know God's deep secrets? To gain more knowledge and understanding of His Word is priceless!

Remember Eve? Read Genesis 3. For a quick review, please see Genesis 3:6.

Eve wanted to be wise, in the wrong way. We know what happened when she ate the forbidden fruit. Sin! All because she wanted to become just like God, knowing everything.

We cannot become gods. If we try to take God's place, the result will be ruin. However, we can gain knowledge, and we can reflect God's own character more and more in our lives. God sent His Son Jesus and now through the Holy Spirit, His Word will be revealed to those who seek Him. When we seek His truth, our relationship with Jesus becomes

Once you get a taste of how sweet God's goodness is, you'll long for more.

stronger and sweeter. We then become more like Jesus in the way we live and in the things we do. We become a reflection of Him.

A personal relationship with Jesus Christ is the key to godliness and true knowledge and wisdom. I pray He is revealing this to you as much as He is to me. It's so exciting! It is through loving Him and loving others that we gain.

Let me remind you of Jesus's words.

"If you don't go all the way with me, through thick and thin, you don't deserve me. If your first concern is to look after yourself, you'll never find yourself. But if you forget about yourself and look to me, you'll find both yourself and me. We are intimately linked in this harvest work. Anyone who accepts what you do, accepts me, the One who sent you. Anyone who accepts what I do accepts my Father, who sent me. Accepting a messenger of God is as good as being God's messenger. Accepting someone's help is as good as giving someone help. This is a large work I've called you into, but don't be overwhelmed by it. It's better to start small. Give a cool cup of water to someone who is thirsty, for instance. The smallest act of giving or receiving make you a true apprentice."
—Matthew 10:38–42 (*The Message*)

Reflect back to the times you have served others. Didn't it satisfy you to do something for someone else? And have you noticed the more you serve and love others your heart begins to change?

Think about this! Every time you

- ♥ serve someone else
- ♥ go on a missions trip
- ♥ take a meal to a friend
- ♥ send a card
- ♥ pray for others
- ♥ say hello to someone new
- ♥ give a hug

Cherished

- ♥ give a financial gift for God's work
- ♥ invite someone to your home
- ♥ make a phone call just because
- ♥ encourage someone
- ♥ smile
- ♥ say "I love you"
- ♥ say "I forgive you"
- ♥ ask "will you forgive me?"
- ♥ say "thank you"
- ♥ help someone in need

you are reflecting Jesus.

Every time we make the choice to serve, to give, to love, we reflect Jesus; and every time it feels so good! Not in a prideful way but in a humble, genuine way that comes from desiring to do the right thing. And wouldn't you agree that every time you serve, the more you want to serve?

Here is a simple prayer that you may want to pray . . .

I love You, Lord, and I count it all joy to serve You. Wherever You call me to go, whatever You ask me to do, I pray that I would be obedient and willing to serve. Lord, in the small things and in the big things, help me to recognize each one is important to You. Lord, give me loving eyes so that I become more aware of the needs of those around me. Amen.

Dreams Do Come True!

As I sat listening to the African Children's Choir™ perform at my church, my eyes filled with tears as God reminded me of something a missionary had told me many years earlier: *We are sending missionaries to Africa today but one day the African people will be coming to America as missionaries to share Jesus with us.*

It was prophetic! There it was right in front of me, children from South Africa singing boldly about Jesus Christ. Every word clearly sung with enthusiasm and every step taken with energy and power. There was no doubt these children were passionate about the One they were worshiping Jesus!

There was a flutter in my heart. The fingers of God were flipping through my mind like a card dealer flips through a deck of cards. He was going way back to my childhood dreams and then He stopped. He pulled out the card that read, "God, I dream of going to Africa." I leaned over to my daughters and said, "I'm going to Africa!" I didn't know how or when, but I knew that I would be going to Africa.

You see, when I was younger, maybe in fifth grade, I had a dream, a desire to go to South Africa. I prayed and asked the Lord to send me there if ever He needed me to go. Now many years later God was beginning to answer that prayer and prepare me to go.

For three years following the children's concert I held on to that desire, knowing God would make a way for me to go to Africa. During those years, we had moved to Houston and had joined a new church. Then one day the missions pastor of our new church called me and asked if I could come in and talk with him about a mission opportunity. I responded, "Is now a good time?" He said "Come on over."

As he shared this opportunity with me, once again my eyes filled with tears of praise and gratitude. His team needed someone to go and speak on sexual purity to about 9,000 students in South Africa! Can you believe it! I wanted to jump up and give the Lord a shout of praise, but I contained myself. Instead my heart filled with joy and tears dropped from my eyes. I sure wanted to! Six weeks later I was on my way to South Africa.

God's timing is amazing! When things aren't happening as fast as you want or maybe they just aren't happening at all, believe me when I tell you, it's all for good. God is always at work! Give it time. Let Him work out the details.

Read Proverbs 3:5–6.

There is nothing greater than knowing you are right where God wants you to be. It's a place of complete peace. In those moments you can't

God's timing is amazing! When things aren't happening as fast as you want or maybe they just aren't happening at all, believe me when I tell you, it's all for good. God is always at work!

Cherished

help but recognize it's nothing you have done, but it's all about what God has set into motion. You can't take any credit nor do you want to. Now the choice is yours. Will you go? God desires for *you* to be a willing vessel so He can pour Himself out. Awesome!

Working as a Team

Don't be selfish; don't try to impress others. Be humble, thinking of others as better than yourselves. Don't look out only for your own interests, but take an interest in others, too.
—Philippians 2:3–4

When God opens the door for you to go on a mission trip you will most probably work with a team. The verse above puts everything into perspective and gives so much wisdom! When you work on a team you must be interested in what the others are doing and what their needs are. Having this attitude unifies any group. Think about it. Sports, cheer and dance teams, swim teams, choirs, youth group trips, school trips, marriage, basically any time you work with another person you become a team. Satan knows that if he can get the team members working against each other, the greater purpose will be lost. Problems within the group can suck the joy right out of what God wants to do in and through you.

Do you remember a time when you had a positive experience working on a team? What about a negative experience? What was the difference?

When you make the decision to go and do whatever He calls you to do, go with *agape* eyes. Here I'm using the Greek word *agape* to mean selfless love felt by Christians for their fellow human beings. This mind-set will enable you to go with a servant's heart. You can't help notice the people God places at every corner and in every moment. How humbling to focus on their needs and not your own. You don't consciously think about it, it's supernatural! God in you! These are divine moments!

The team God put together for my South Africa missions trip was wonderful! No doubt, it was handpicked by Him personally. When you serve the Lord together and pray for one another, you become close. You love each other as brothers and sisters in Christ. Like a tapestry being woven together, it took each of our gifts, talents, and obedience to accomplish the mission. Perhaps the closeness of these new relationships is a gift from God—His favor on His children for working so well together to accomplish His purpose.

As we began to go out and meet the people, I noticed right away the words *rich* and *poor* take on different meanings when you're doing God's work. Although the people we were ministering to were economically poor—living in makeshift homes from garbage found on the road—many of them were rich in spirit. Hmmm, doesn't that match what Jesus taught us in Luke 16? Being rich or poor depends on the condition of your heart not how much money you have. These people, though they have little, have much joy! Believe me, since *joy* is my favorite word I recognize it quickly or notice the lack thereof.

Each day we would pull up to townships (or squatters' camps) where the people hurried over to our van. Children followed us through the walkways between the small homes to make sure they didn't miss anything we had to share. The children were so excited to receive a simple sticker that read *Jesus loves me* or *God is love*. Most of the adults wanted one too!

Once everyone had been invited we began our program. We sang about Jesus, and they sang with us enthusiastically and loudly! When we shared a Bible story, they listened intently. When we shared the good news of Jesus Christ and how He loves them and has a plan for their life and that He is preparing a new home for them in heaven, the people quickly responded. When we passed out Bibles in their language, they couldn't wait to hold one tightly to their chest, like a treasure or a priceless

♥

Being rich or poor depends on the condition of your heart not how much money you have.

Cherished

gift. At some of the places we visited we didn't give each person a Bible, but instead gave some as a gift for answered questions. While packing up to leave one time I noticed a young lady who had received a Bible with seven other girls around her as she read from the pages. I thought to myself: *How sad that some people have Bibles in their home that sit on shelves or lay on tables but are never opened and certainly not treasured.* Don't take your Bible for granted. Read it. Care for it. It's the Word of God!

The students, teachers, children, and parents at each stop were eager to hear what we had to share about Jesus. They need the hope of Jesus just as everyone does. No matter where you live or what your house looks like, we all go through desperate times in life when we come to our wit's end, a place of total surrender. When you can't do anything else, trust that Jesus will do it for you. Isn't it wonderful to know God's Word transcends all generations and cultures. *"Jesus Christ is the same yesterday and today and forever"* (Hebrews 13:8 NIV). God's Word is the Truth! Jesus is the Way! That will never change!

Here is some of a letter I wrote to my prayer supporters when I returned home from South Africa.

♥ ♥ ♥

Thank you so much for praying for me and my family while I was away. What an incredible trip! God is so good and this will be a highlight of my life...for sure!

I spoke on abstinence (straight talk from God's Word) in ten schools to thousands of students. There are just no words to describe it. Just know that God was and is at work, and we saw many make decisions. It's not the numbers that are important, but each life that was changed. The Lord knows the hearts of the students, and we praise Him for the opportunity to share His Truth! Praise You Jesus!

If you could only hear the voices of the South African people...when they pray, oh they pray. When they sing, oh they worship! When they listen, oh they listen with everything within them! Try to imagine 1,200 African students at one time jumping and smiling and praising Jesus.

There is one face I'll never forget. We were at a very poor school. All the children there live in squatters camps…no running water, no bathrooms, dirt for floors, and most have lost parents to AIDS (some of the children have it as well). On this day, just as I said let us pray (actually I was going to pray aloud *for* them), they all began to pray the Lord's Prayer out loud in unison. On the front row, a little boy, probably six years old, clasped his hands tightly together and as he intently addressed "our Father who art in heaven," it was as though he was looking into the face of God. I thought to myself how often I have said the words, but sadly at times they were just memorized words without any meaning. May the Lord forgive me if I ever say this prayer again without praying it earnestly.

I praise You, O Lord, for the opportunity You gave to share Your truth and salvation with those in South Africa. Continue to bless and provide for the pastor and his church as they reach out with food and water to those who are hungry. And as they share with each one who comes into the doors of that place that *"Salvation is found in no one else, for there is no other name under heaven given to man by which we must be saved"* (Acts 4:12 NIV).

Counting it all joy to serve my Jesus,
Chandra Peele

♥ ♥ ♥

Victory in Jesus

Only a day after we left, some of the townships we'd visited in were under attack. Some of the "local" people were angry at those in the townships because they felt these "squatters" were taking jobs away from them. Tragically, when people are hungry and have no money, they do desperate things. A gang of the locals, called "the ring of fire," literally burn people alive. They invaded some of the camps we had just ministered in.

♥

I praise You, O Lord, for the opportunity You gave to share Your truth and salvation with those in South Africa.

Cherished

Girls, life isn't always pretty. It certainly isn't always "happy." However, we can have joy in the midst of the pain when we have Jesus as our Comforter, our Shield, our Hope, our Rock, our Provider, our Lord, and our Savior.

Hearing about this horrific situation in South Africa grieves my spirit. However, we who belong to Christ are victorious! Do you understand that? Do you believe that in your own life?

What does it mean for you to be victorious in every situation and how is this possible?

Read the Scriptures below and after each one write your thoughts. How do these verses relate to the people in South Africa and to you here in America?

They were at their wits' end. Then they cried out to the LORD in their trouble, and he brought them out of their distress.
—Psalm 107:27–28 (NIV)

I am willing to endure anything if it will bring salvation and eternal glory in Christ Jesus to those God has chosen.
—2 Timothy 2:10

And this same God who takes care of me will supply all your needs from his glorious riches, which have been given to us in Christ Jesus.
—Philippians 4:19

Do Not Fear

What is God calling you to do? Many who are called never go because of fear. It's not hard to see that this is Satan's plan to keep you from being used by God. Don't let fear trap you. Fear is one of Satan's favorite tools. God tell us, *"Do not be afraid, for I am with you"* (Isaiah 43:5 NIV).

Read Exodus 2:7–8.

Fear will keep you from God-sized opportunities. What are some things you have missed out on because of fear?

Read Luke 9:24–25.

Don't be fearful of death.
Can you see how you will gain life if you surrender to Jesus?

What good is it to gain the whole world but lose your soul?

It's no good at all! Think about it and write your thoughts.

Gain the World   Lose Your Soul

Which one will you choose?

If God calls you to go, wherever that may be, go! It is better to serve the Lord and be obedient than to stay behind and be disobedient.

I personally have never known anyone who was serving the Lord who wished they had not done so. Those who have gone before you will agree that if you are in God's will you're able to trust whatever happens will be according to His purpose. There is peace that comes with obedience. *"You will keep in perfect peace all who trust in you, all whose thoughts are fixed on you!"* (Isaiah 26:3).

Did you know that faith most often comes out of a fearful moment? Have you had something come up you didn't expect that frightened you, caused fear to rise up in you, such as illness, the death of a loved one, an accident, etc.? Perhaps a test you were unprepared for? Perhaps not having enough money to pay some bills that you knew were coming due soon? How did these situations make you feel? What happened?

Desperate people do desperate things. In what way does desperation fuel fear?

Read Matthew 14:24–31.

Think about your own fears. Do you sometimes feel that you too are being pushed to "walk on water?"

Compare your fear to Peter's. What fear do you have that is equivalent to walking on water?

What can you or did you learn from your fearful situation?

In what way do you think it brought you back to faith or perhaps made your faith in the Lord stronger?

I know in my own life fear has often been the factor that pushed me to faith. In those times my faith grew, and my relationship with the Lord became more intimate. During each of these experiences I had no control, therefore I learned to put my total trust in the Lord and depend on Him. This is faith. It should come as no surprise that the Father will allow us to come to a place of desperation so we will draw closer to Him. The next time fear rises up in you, remember that fear often leads us to faith and faith always leads us to the arms of our heavenly Father.

Do you know someone who lives everyday by faith? Explain your reason for thinking of this particular person. Has her example encouraged you to life by faith?

Have there been times when you or your family had faith in God to provide or help you during a painful, desperate season of life? What happened? Did this experience bring glory to God? Write your thoughts.

God has called us to live in freedom, not to live in fear. So live life enthusiastically! Serve God every time the opportunity arises! And encourage someone else to live by faith.

Cherished

GAB Session
~ with Chandra ~

Are You Ready to Serve?

What? You don't have time? Oh girl, we need to talk!

I'm really good at making plans and filling up my calendar. In fact, if you opened my calendar you might think I've got my whole life planned out, or at least the next year. But God is working on me. I'm beginning to realize that being a God follower means I should be more than flexible, I need to be fluid. Let me explain. Flexible is good. That means the plan can change and you don't get out of sorts…instead you make adjustments without flipping out. Being fluid means that you basically live from moment to moment. Like a wave in the ocean or a ripple on a lake, you just go with the flow of what God is doing. You still may have a calendar, but you hold those plans loosely, being ready to move when the unexpected happens or better yet, when God-sized opportunity comes.

I'm praying you don't miss a thing God has for you. Riding the wave of His goodness and mercy…well, there's just nothing better. One of the sweetest blessings is that you begin to see, hear, and know God more. This journey is amazing! Don't miss out! And don't keep waiting. Start today!

Pray that you will begin to notice where and when God is working. Pray that you will hear Him when He calls you. Pray that God will move you or move in you until He takes you to that place of total surrender. All for your good and for His best!

We know that God causes everything to work together for the good of those who love God and are called according to his purpose for them.
—Romans 8:28

No one is good—except God alone.
—Mark 10:18 (NIV)

When we read these verses we can see how the focus should be off our-selves and on God alone. God is the Famous One. God is on the throne. God is the only One who should be in the spotlight.

The next time you have a prideful moment—you get your feelings hurt because no one noticed the good job you did or perhaps a friend always gets the attention instead of you—just remember to shine the light back on Jesus. He's the only One that deserves it anyway. The more you understand His love, His grace, His mercy, and all that He did for you on the cross, you won't be able to hide it! You can't contain some-thing of that magnitude! It won't be long until you begin to reflect Him outwardly for all to see.

That's another thing I love about missions. Pride is cast aside, and it's about others. It's about serving and giving and loving; it's about loving God with all our heart and soul and mind and loving others as we love ourselves. Our reward is to hear Him say, *"Well done, good and faithful ser-vant!"* (Matthew 25:21 NIV).

It is my prayer that this session has given you a snapshot of what serving others looks like. I pray my description of the faces I've seen and the excitement in my heart and theirs made an impression on your mind. You know there are just some facial expressions you can't forget, like the look of someone who has just been surprised or the reaction of a child who has just been licked in the face by a puppy. Imagine the expres-sion on the face of God when His children show His love by serving one another. Can you see it?

Sometimes when my heart is full of joy and I'm so grateful to God my Father I simply look up, close my eyes, and try my best to envision His face. One day I will see Him face to face and, oh, what a day that will be! But until then, I willingly, wholeheartedly desire to love, serve, and obey in expectation of "that day" when we meet face to face.

Take a moment and get somewhere comfortable. Think about all you have read and just be still, be quiet. Wait patiently and you will hear

Cherished

from the Lord. Perhaps the Lord will show you some new things, a new path, a new you. Then spend some time with the Lord in prayer. You can say the prayer I have written or say your own.

My Prayer

Lord, I get so excited just thinking about the day I will see Your face. Until that day I can only love You and love others because I know that is what pleases You. Lord, I can't help but smile when I imagine Your face. The warmth I feel all around me from my head to my toes must be Your perfect and complete love for me. Lord, when Your love fills me up it makes me so ready to serve someone else. Cast out all fear in me and help me to have faith to trust in You alone. Lead me, Lord, to who You would have me serve, even today. I don't want to miss the opportunity to serve others, so I pray that You would open the doors in my home, my family, my neighborhood, my school, my church, my community…and that I would be faithful to walk through them. Amen.

My Journal

So what do you think? Are you ready to serve? Have the stories in this session caused you think about going on a mission trip or visiting a nursing home? Are you more concerned about people who don't know the Father?

~~~~~~

~~~~~~

Have any big dreams? You never know what God has in your future, so never stop dreaming. Your dreams just might come true. Remember Ephesians 3:20?

~~~~~~

~~~~~~

~~~~~~

~~~~~~

~~~~~~

~~~~~~

~~~~~~

~~~~~~

~~~~~~

~~~~~~

Cherished

Freedom to Love and Be Loved

Jesus replied, "'You must love the LORD your God with all your heart, all your soul, and all your mind.' This is the first and greatest commandment. A second is equally important: 'Love your neighbor as yourself.'"
—Matthew 22:37–39

Are you ready? Ready to love God and others more than ever before? After reading Matthew 22:37–39 many times over during this study, you certainly have a greater understanding of God and these two commandments. Now you can see why His focus is on your heart, your mind, and your soul. There He can see the *real* you! And now that you realize who you *really* are is found on the inside, you're aware that your *inside* greatly influences your *outside*.

What do you look like on the inside right now, this very moment? Have you allowed negative thoughts and words from others to knock down your spirit? Have you heard someone talk ugly about you or be critical of you? If so, don't sit there and continue to replay these hurtful actions over and over. No! Stand up straight, shake it off, and reprogram your thoughts. Put them back on track, onto thoughts that reflect God. Your thoughts should be more like this: I am a child of God; I am fearfully and wonderfully made; I am blessed; I am cherished; I am smart; I am talented; I am able to change my direction; I am running

Now you can see why His focus is on your heart, your mind, and your soul. There He can see the real you!

this race and I will finish strong; I am loved by God my Father who watches over me; I will not let this get me down. Don't say these words of affirmation out of arrogance, but in a quiet confidence given to you by the Spirit of God.

If you continue to let words, people, and your past hurt you, your inside may never heal and you may never live your life to your fullest potential. God's plan for each of us is to live an abundant life. To live with joy! To live in freedom! To experience life to its fullest! God never promised life would always be easy and that we would never encounter problems, but He did promise He would always be with us. It's how we go through life's experiences that makes us weaker or stronger. I've recognized in my good times and in my bad that my mind-set determines my outlook. Let me ask you a question. When given the choice between good, better, or best, which will you choose? Sadly, some settle for good when God has so much more waiting for them. Some feel that they aren't deserving of the best. My friend, none of us deserve eternal life, but by God's grace it is given to us! Don't settle for the good life; instead, get ready for the best that God has planned for you!

Let's Talk about Mind-set
Example #1
You were late to school, your hair looked horrible, your friend shared your secret with others, you don't have money for the game this Friday night, and your zipper just broke on your jeans.

Based on the fact that you are living your life according to Matthew 22:37–39, how would you handle this kind of a day?

♥

God never promised life would always be easy and that we would never encounter problems, but He did promise He would always be with us.

Cherished

Example #2

You had a great day! You passed the test with an A+, or perhaps you got the C you desperately needed. You were named employee of the month. Your team won the game, and you were humbled by the applause. You felt good on the inside; your quiet time with the Lord started your day off great. You have a smile on your face and a positive outlook on life. Everyone liked your new outfit, and it was even a good hair day! You helped a friend, fed the dog, and sent your grandmother a card. Today was a rainbow kind of day!

Based on the fact that you are living your life according to Matthew 22:37–39 how would you handle this kind of a day?

Now it's your turn to describe your day.
My day was:

Based on the fact that you are living your life according to Matthew 22:37–39, how did you handle this kind of day?

To encourage myself today I should say: I am_____.

On a piece of paper write down something that represents any negative thought that has been stuck to you like glue. After you write it, crumple the page, and throw it away. Ask the Lord to help you get back on track; ask Him to replace the negative thoughts in your mind with positive ones. If you had a day more like the person in example #1, what was something positive about your day and how did it make you feel?

If your day was more like the girl in example #2, was there a moment that you may have missed serving someone else? Or could it be that you became prideful or arrogant, which made others feel badly?

You've thought about how you are feeling on the inside. Now consider how you're doing on the outside today. Your attitude. Your actions. You know…your life.

I guess the best way to put it is this: When someone looked at you today, what did they see?

Someone who

- ♥ is discouraged and defeated.
- ♥ angry and confused.
- ♥ mean, rude, and inconsiderate of others.
- ♥ never smiles.
- ♥ has a chip on her shoulders.
- ♥ had a bad day but didn't let it defeat her.
- ♥ didn't win the game but congratulated those who did.
- ♥ doesn't like what's happening at the moment but knows tomorrow is a new day.
- ♥ hasn't had a lot of support but dreams of a greater future.
- ♥ says "God, I don't know what's going on, but I know You do and I'm going to trust You!"

Throughout the Bible there are stories that can encourage us, no matter what we are going through. Joseph, David, Daniel, Ruth, and Mary were young people who faced difficulties and challenges.

I'm sure you have it by now. Jesus modeled Matthew 22:37–39 in His life and now we should model our life after His. Jesus desires the best for us, and He knows that if we love God first with our heart, mind, and soul, then life will be much sweeter. He knows that if we serve those in need and put others in front of ourselves, then our hearts will be full of love and joy. He knows that only when we love Him and serve others will we be free to love who we are.

Throughout the Bible there are stories that can encourage us, no mat-

Cherished

ter what we are going through. Joseph, David, Daniel, Ruth, and Mary were young people who faced difficulties and challenges. The Bible is practical. It's not *if* you encounter problems, it's *when* you encounter problems. The Word of God doesn't say *if* you grieve, it says *when* you grieve. The Bible doesn't say *if* people hurt you, it says *when* people hurt you.

The Father knows that, in difficult times and in good times, we all need to be loved and we all need to give love to one another. How you handle problems, your choices, your integrity—basically your overall character—will influence the people around you. Psalm 55:22 says: *"Give your burdens to the Lord, and he will take care of you. He will not permit the godly to slip and fall."*

Stop here and pray that God will make you more aware of what is on the inside and what shines through to the outside. Pray that you will reflect Him more and more.

Isn't it amazing how the inside and the outside feed off each other? It's pretty obvious, right? The voices, the words, the leftover negative junk that is stuck on the inside will continue to suck us dry, causing us to focus all our energy on the junk rather than on God. And this mind-set will certainly keep our thoughts on us and not on others.

Can you give an example over the last few weeks of some "junk" in your own life?

Did you shake it off or did it consume your thoughts?

Of God's truths that we've studied so far, which have been most relevant and applicable to your life recently?

On the other hand, maybe you have had very little negative in your life but a lot of positive. You have been encouraged through words and actions by family, teachers, and friends, and life is going smoothly. Remember, you shouldn't be puffed up and conceited about your blessings, instead you should pay it forward, pass it on. Have you? Are you?

Give an example of something positive that has happened to you during the past few weeks. Did that good experience motivate you to help others? Did your positive feelings overflow to bless others? You can respond by asking yourself how you treated others, served others, and went through your daily routine.

Write your response.

New Again

Funny, but the first thing that comes to my mind when I consider the inside of something overflowing to the outside is a car, a particular car. Have you ever known anyone who has rebuilt an old car? I do. Our friend, Donnie, bought a car that looked like a piece of junk. This old car was rusted inside and out, it smelled terrible, and it didn't even run! But Donnie was determined to put her back together and make her look like new again. The reason I say her is that he even gave the car a name, "Nadine." Donnie and some friends took Nadine completely apart, literally. Every screw, nut, and bolt, every big and little piece, all the seats…everything! Then he began to rebuild Nadine after work and on the weekends and on his days off for years. Finally, Nadine came to life. Girls, I must say, she is one hot lady! She's a '56 Chevy that looks like she just came off the assembly line: vintage turquoise and white paint, beautiful white leather interior, and all the bells and whistles you could request back in the day.

Cherished

Talk about a lady that will turn your head. She's definitely one!

Donnie had a dream, a real heart's desire, to rebuild this old car. He pictured it in his mind and believed that one day he would be sitting at the local drive-in ordering his dinner on a double date. After all the blood, sweat, and tears, everyone knew that this old car was something really special to him. So let me ask you a question. Do you think he keeps her outside in the rain, puts the cheapest gas in her he can find, and only glances at her every now and then? I don't think so! Au contraire. Nadine is treated like a queen bee. I won't go so far as to say Donnie loves this car, but believe me, he takes good care of her. She'll get the proper grade of gas, her oil will be changed when needed, the tires will have the proper amount of air in them, and she'll stay clean as a whistle. And there's no doubt Donnie will have a smile on his face every time he takes her out for a spin.

Let's consider your spiritual life. Are you a mess on the inside and in need of someone to rescue you? Has this study shaken your core? Has it perhaps loosened up some of those rusty bolts that have been barely holding your heart together? Donnie rescued the old car and restored her. My sweet sister, God wants to rescue you, to clean you up inside and out, to clothe you with His righteousness, and fill you up with His Spirit. Then when He sends you out, oh how He will smile knowing you are beautiful and shining bright for Him!

Now that we are in the last session of our study I hope you will stop and consider what God has done for you during these past weeks. When you began, maybe you felt like your life was out of control or out of commission, like that old car in the junkyard. But God found you and brought you into *His* garage. Weak and frail, lonely and confused, you were the one He chose to bring in out of the storms. Maybe you felt the grip of His strong hands take you apart, then gently and slowly restore you one piece at a time. Who knows, it could be that you're still in the process of being taken apart and cleaned up. Maybe you had a few specific maintenance needs. Junk in the trunk? Grime in the mind? An engine that was burned up and had no life, no joy? But now you have a new confidence.

My sweet sister, God wants to rescue you, to clean you up inside and out, to clothe you with His righteousness, and fill you up with His Spirit.

No matter which part of the process you are in today, isn't it good to know you are a work in progress? There's something happening with you—a change taking place on the inside. You've been cleaned up and you're ready to shine! Others are turning to check you out, taking notice, because there is something different about you these days. They see a reflection of someone, but it's not the old you. Could it be? Yes, I think it is. They see a reflection of Jesus! In your smile, in your actions, in your attitude, and in your willingness to serve, they see love! An indisputable heartfelt love! You can't help but smile, because you can't contain it! This new love is bubbling up from within, and it's contagious! Your family, your friends, the stranger you meet on the street, they look different to you. You are humbled as you know full well that it is by His presence in your life that you are being made new. This is it! You've got it! Loving Him, loving others, and finally understanding what it means to love yourself. This is freedom!

Read John 1:12–13.

How do these verses relate to the car story?
I'll give you a hint: "Made new." At what stage are you in the car story?

Read Psalm 126.

Be encouraged!

Who's Pouring into You?

Like gas in any car, it's important to know what or who we allow to fill us up. God's Word, the Bible, is a Christian's greatest source for a good fill-up and a must to keep us running well spiritually. We also need to

Cherished

recognize that people pour into our lives and what others pour in will determine what our mind, heart, and soul pours out. For this reason it's good to have a routine maintenance check to be sure who is pouring into you.

Who is pouring into your life today?

Let's start with those who influenced your life when you were younger. Who are those who left lasting impressions on your life?

When I think about those who poured into me I am so very thankful!

For me, a few come to mind immediately. In fact, there are many who poured their love into me during my teen years, probably close to your age. As I look back over my life, I can see that God appointed some people to press godly principles and wisdom into the very core of my heart. I was blessed to have a godly mother and father, and for them I am forever grateful! Yes, I remember them teaching me to treat others nicely and to say "thank you" and "you're welcome." I remember my mom saying, "Chandra, don't interrupt." But I also learned so much from the way they loved each other and through the way they loved me. I remember waiting for my daddy to come home after work (which was eleven at night) and move me from my parents' bed to my own, bedtime prayers and a blessing at every meal, Wednesday night suppers at church and singing old hymns, Sunday morning church, roast for lunch, and back by five-thirty. Youth group and mission trips, singing in the youth choir, and Sunday night fellowships. When I think about those who poured into me I am so very thankful!

♥ ♥ ♥

Here are three of the most important principles I learned from early influencers.

The Bible is God's Word.

When I was in third grade, my Sunday school teacher, Mrs. Stovall, gave me a beautiful white Bible for my birthday. She had my name printed in gold on the front cover, and I was so proud! Every Sunday we had a Bible drill, and I remember flipping quickly through the pages from the Old Testament to the New Testament. Mrs. Stovall taught me that there are 66 books in the Bible: 39 in the Old Testament and 27 in the New Testament. She taught me a song to help us remember the order of the books of the Bible, and I still hum it today when I can't find my way. I remember how Mrs. Stovall prayed and how she dressed—usually in a suit, beauty-shop hair, and always a soft, sweet smile on her face. Many loved her because she loved everyone! Today, that white Bible she gave me has a special place on a bookshelf in my office. I will always cherish the memory of Mrs. Stovall, who gave me a love for God's Word.

> *For the word of God is alive and powerful. It is sharper than the sharpest two-edged sword, cutting between soul and spirit, between joint and marrow. It exposes our innermost thoughts and desires.*
> —Hebrews 4:12

God is love. He cares for the whole world.

The first female speaker I recall hearing was Mildred McWhorter. I thought she was famous! I grew up going to Girls in Action camp, and she was always our speaker. Each year there was a different camp theme, but her message was always the same; "God is love and we should love every tribe, every nation, and every neighbor." She also ran the Southern Baptist Mission Home in downtown Houston, where I lived. We would often go help out at the mission home: clean up, size clothes, refill or organize the food pantry, serve food to the homeless. Ms. Mildred was full of Jesus *and* she was funny! She talked about Jesus like He was her closest friend. I remember thinking, *I hope one day I can know Jesus like that!* I can hear her now, "You can just talk to Jesus like He's sitting right here beside you." Ms. Mildred, what a precious lady! She was a role model for me. When she gets to heaven, I'm sure the people will be lining up to thank her for telling them about this wonderful Jesus, the Messiah! She gave her life serving others. She taught me so much about being a Christ follower, because she lived it.

Do nothing out of selfish ambition or vain conceit, but in humility consider others better than yourselves. Each of you should look not only to your own interests but also to the interests of others. Your attitude should be the same as that of Christ Jesus.
—Philippians 2:3–5 (NIV)

Jesus gives us joy.

Wanda Kipp is the woman who taught me about the joy of the Lord. "JOY: Jesus, others, and then yourself," she would say. *Joy* is my favorite word, and Ms. Wanda's JOY acronym is a great reminder of Matthew 22:37–39. She also taught me that Christians should have more fun than anyone because they have the joy of Jesus deep in their hearts. She had a contagious laugh. Have you ever known anyone like that? They laugh and something about it makes everyone else laugh too. Her smile was simply an expression of God's love.

I know this is a strange thing to mention, but I also loved how she wrote my name. I remember I practiced until I had it down. I still write my name like that today. The *C* is larger than the rest of the letters and swoops down below.

She taught me that personality and character are more important than what people see on the outside. "A person's eyes and smile tell you a lot about the person," she said. Ms. Wanda was a friend of many.

"I have told you this so that my joy may be in you and that your joy may be complete."
—John 15:11 (NIV)

♥ ♥ ♥

Now think about your own life. Who are those who have pressed into you godly principles, standards, and morals? Write your thoughts down as I have. As you think about these influential people, can you see how God put them in your path to help shape you into the young woman you have become today?

List others who have influenced your life.
(Coaches, teachers, parent of a friend, friends, etc.)

♥

Can you see how these people love God and through that love have shown love to you?

Often the best example of God's love is found right in front of you or when you least expect it. Some who have had an influence on your life may not be Christians.

What action could you take to show God's love to them?

Cherished

Read Romans 12:9–13.

Don't just pretend that you love others. Really love them. Hate what is wrong. Hold tightly to what is good. Love each other with genuine affection, and take delight in honoring each other. Never be lazy, but work hard and serve the Lord enthusiastically. Rejoice in our confident hope. Be patient in trouble, and keep on praying. When God's people are in need, be ready to help them out. Always be eager to practice hospitality.

Break these verses down. Consider how you can apply these verses to love others today.

The Prayer that Changed My Life

OK, hold on to your seats, because this story is one of my favorites! When I was 23 years old I went to my first "ladies" conference. A group of us went together from my church, and we were all very excited! After introductions and worship through music, the main speaker took the stage. I quickly became interested in all that she was saying. Then it happened—a moment that would change my life forever! As I focused on her so intently something unexplainable happened. It was as though I was the only one in the room and it was me on the stage instead of her. The words were hers, but I was seeing my body and hearing my voice. I can't tell you what she was saying, however, I know God was speaking to me. This was the second time in my life that I had a vision from the Lord.

The first time I had a vision from the Lord occurred during a youth camp, when I was 16. I felt God call me to ministry. Though it's hard to put into words, I knew with my heart and soul that God wanted me to serve Him through full-time ministry. I just didn't have any details.

♥

Though it's hard to put into words, I knew with my heart and soul that God wanted me to serve Him through full-time ministry.

How? I did not know. When? No idea. I just knew to be looking for opportunities to serve and that is what I did.

Back to the ladies conference. I had been praying for seven years for God to show me how He wanted me to serve Him with my vocation. He answered me when I least expected it. Not wanting my friends to think I was strange or anything, I didn't share the vision with them, but I knew I needed to meet this speaker! Not knowing how that would be possible with a crowd of a thousand or so women, I simply prayed, "Lord, if you want me to meet her You will make a way."

During the break, the lines at the restrooms were really long, so I decided to wait until the end of the break and slip out then. When I came out of the restroom stall, I could hardly believe my eyes. There was the speaker washing her hands at the sink. OK, I thought, this might be awkward. The poor lady may think, *Goodness gracious, I can't even go to the ladies room without someone wanting to talk to me!* Well, I didn't let that stop me. I seized the moment!

After telling her how much I was enjoying her message, I introduced myself. Then the rest just rolled out of my mouth.

"As you were speaking, I believe the Lord answered my prayer," I said. "Called to ministry at 16, I've been praying that He would show me what it is He has called me to do. While I was listening to you speak, He told me! God wants me to speak and encourage ladies to live for Him like you do."

I remember trembling as I spoke. She smiled and held my hand, then she placed her other hand on my shoulder and she prayed. "Lord, as this sister seeks to do Your will we believe that You will guide her steps and lead her to that place. We trust You, Lord, and look forward to all You will accomplish through her obedience. Step by step, Lord. Amen."

With a quick hug she said, "I must go. I'll be on stage in just a few moments. God bless you!" I remember it all so clearly.

A couple years ago, about 20 years after this conference experience, I received a call inviting me to speak at an event in Tennessee. By this time, I'd been traveling and speaking for several years. The week before the event, the event coordinator called me to go over final details. She informed me that I would be speaking on Sunday to both the girls and the ladies. The schedule called for everyone to come together on Sunday morning for worship and a closing message from both the ladies speaker and the student speaker. She mentioned the name of the other speaker and I stopped her to make sure I had the name correct.

"Who will be speaking to the ladies?" I asked.

"Esther Burroughs," she answered.

My heart almost leaped through the phone! It was Esther Burroughs who had prayed with me in the ladies room those many years ago. Often I had asked the Lord to allow our paths to cross again. Now He was answering my prayer in a wonderful way. I could hardly wait to share my story with her. To hug her and thank her for taking time to say a one-minute prayer with me that would forever change my life!

In our first meeting, Mrs. Burroughs could have used the excuse that she was speaking in less than five minutes and needed to get back to the stage quickly. She could have thought my timing was very inconvenient. Though she *was* busy and my timing *was* inconvenient, she seized the moment anyway and greatly influenced my life. This was God's love in action! This was wonderful! No one could ever take credit for this? No one but God!

I did go to Tennessee and meet Esther Burroughs for the second time. What a joy to share with her how God had answered the prayer she prayed years earlier for my life. I saw God in her when we met that day in the restroom years ago. I saw Him again when we met 20 years later. A life touched by God always ends in touching others. Now I've been traveling and speaking to groups for almost ten years, loving and thanking God for each opportunity!

What may look like an inconvenience to us might be no less than the beginning of a life-changing opportunity. We should never underestimate the importance of one moment, one word, one deed in the life of another human being. Jesus Christ is our greatest example of influence! Not only did He have amazing influence on those who walked with Him on earth, He continues to reach into the hearts and souls of men and women across the world, changing us from the inside out. It's a miracle!

A life touched by God always ends in touching others.

Think about those you are influencing. Can you name some of them and describe how your influence can make a difference in their lives?

But anyone who does not love does not know God, for God is love.
—1 John 4:8

Dear friends, since God loved us that much, we surely ought to love each other. No one has ever seen God. But if we love each other, God lives in us, and his love is brought to full expression through us.
—1 John 4:11–12

Take a moment to break these two verses down line-by-line and study them. Repeat them and memorize them. Apply them to your life. 1 John 4:11 really sums up our study, doesn't it?

In Good Times and Bad

I hope you can testify how wonderful it is to be loved by God and how wonderful it is to share God's love with others. And those times when you know that God used another person to speak truth and wisdom to you…it's just awesome! It's exciting to share what God has done for us in the good times. How He has blessed us, answered our prayers, cared for us and provided for us.

But it's also important to consider His love for us in times of trouble and loss. Some of you reading this may be going through a rough time even now. During these low times of life, valleys some call them, God is at work. Remember, you are free to choose how you will go through this valley. Emotionally, you may experience many different feelings. You can feel angry; you can cry until the tears are dried up; you can run away from

God; you can fall into His loving arms. God's love is the same every minute of every day, in the good times as well as the seemingly bad times.

Have you been there in the valleys? If not, perhaps you know someone else who has gone through or is now in a valley. When others are hurting, we should be quick to show God's love to them. It's normal not to know what to say or how to respond when someone else is going through a hard time. When this happens, hug them, send a card, and let them know you are praying for them. Have you ever noticed how Christians embrace those who are sick in the hospital, going through cancer, or mourning when a loved one has passed away? I've seen this many times in my life and have experienced it personally. God's people seem to swing into action when others are hurting. These touches of love, they bring glory to God. They show we love God and we love others.

To love and to be loved . . . we need both in our life.

Whose love is constant in your life?

Who has shown you love today?

Who are you showing God's love to today?

Maybe you are at a place in your spiritual life where loving others comes naturally and you see opportunities to love all around you. Write your thoughts as if you were sharing your story with a friend. Be sure to include where this love is coming from.

God's people seem to swing into action when others are hurting. These touches of love, they bring glory to God.

Do you know someone who is hurting? What will your response be to them?

My Prayer

Almighty Father, You are worthy of all my praise in every situation. Lord, when I don't understand the hows and whys of painful times in my life, I know that I can trust You. Thank You, Jesus, that during these times I can rest in the arms of Your amazing and never-ending love. Lord, for those who are hurting today, help me to be sensitive to their needs. Lord, if one of my friends is hurting, I pray the Holy Spirit will speak to me and guide me to know what to say or what to do. Lord, You have called me to love, so that is exactly what I want to do. Give me the desire to step out and do something, perhaps out of my comfort zone, so that others will see Your love through my actions. Thank You for saving me and thank You for the promise and hope of eternal life. Thank You for Jesus and it's in His name I pray. Amen.

Cherished

GAB Session
~~with Chandra ~~

Walking Through the Valley

I have to say there are times when I struggle to find time for God. That just sounds awful, doesn't it? How could a person be too busy for God? Well, not to make excuses, but I think maybe you know what I mean. Then there are times in my life when I feel as though I'm on a river raft with God. Life is moving along smoothly, and I'm talking, laughing, and sharing deep thoughts with my heavenly Father as He sits right beside me. At those times, I am free from doubt, worry, and the problems of this world, because I know He's in control of my life. It's a good place to be!

Let me share about a time in my life when God was there for me in a very frightening situation. We were preparing to move and change seemed to be coming from every direction of my life. For a month, I had opened my Bible first thing every morning. Even during the day I had a craving to read my devotion book or have another look at my Bible. Praying had become an all-day conversation with the Lord because I wanted so much to hear His direction in my life. Well, I did. He answered my prayer and on this particular night I heard Him speak to my heart and His Holy Spirit directed my steps.

It was Tuesday night, May 1, about nine in the evening. Bruce had gone to Houston and I was cleaning out my closet getting ready for a garage sale that weekend. We were moving from San Antonio to Houston the following week. Around ten thirty, Lindsey, my oldest daughter, called and said she was on her way home.

"Hey, Mom. It looks like a storm is coming! It's not raining yet but the lightning is crazy!" she said.

"Well, you be careful, Honey. Hopefully you'll make it home before the rain comes. Love you!"

"Love you too, Mom!" she said.

We talked for a few minutes, and I knew to expect her home in about 15 minutes.

Reeses, our little dog, started barking like she normally does when someone in the family comes home. It had started to rain by this time, and I thought we would greet Lindsey with an open garage door and an umbrella. After waiting a few minutes I called Lindsey to see where she was, and I got no answer. I waited just a few minutes longer and called again.

Though it may seem strange, I felt something inside. I'm sure it was that still, small voice people talk about. I felt guided by the presence of the Holy Spirit and I was calm, but I knew something was terribly wrong. I knew I had to go find my daughter.

I have to stop for a moment and share something before I go on. Since Lindsey had gone off to college two years earlier I always had this sick sense about her getting into an accident. When she came home to visit I would pray for her safety just about nonstop. I always prayed, "Lord, keep her alert as she drives. Don't let my phone calls be a distraction. And Lord, please don't ever let me get the dreaded phone call."

Finally, the Lord took me to a verse in the Bible that gave me comfort. Isaiah 26:3 reads, *"You will keep in perfect peace all who trust in you."* From that time on I had been able to trust the Lord for Lindsey's safety, and I truly had a peace.

OK, back to the story. I got in my car and began to backtrack where I thought she would be driving. The neighborhood where she worked was only about 15 miles from our home. I was calm, yet on a mission to find my daughter. The rain was coming down harder and the lightning lit up the skies like a beacon. Then I saw them: the red flashing lights, a fire truck, an ambulance, and a police car. I began to cry. I knew Lindsey had been in a terrible accident.

As I approached, I saw a little silver car, actually half a silver car. When I got there, the ambulance driver came over and said, "Are you a nurse?"

I said, "No! That's my daughter! Is she OK?"

Cherished

You have to try and imagine this. All I could see was half a car, and the other part was either crushed upward or missing completely, I couldn't tell.

The EMT asked, "How do you know this is your daughter? We just got here moments ago."

I said, "God told me to go, that my daughter needed me."

She asked, "What is your daughter's name?"

I said, as best that I could get out, "Lindsey."

She followed up, "Lindsey Peele?"

That's when I began to shake and cry. It was indeed Lindsey.

The EMT put both her hands on my shoulders and said, "You need to look at me and listen! Lindsey is already in an ambulance and on her way to the hospital. She was unconscious when we arrived on the scene, but before they left with her she was awake and responsive. She is in shock, but I can say that she was moving her arms and legs."

After seeing the wreckage, anyone's first thought would have been: that person didn't survive. As Lindsey pulled out of the neighborhood, what she didn't see was a speeding car coming around the corner at an estimated 97 miles per hour. Lindsey was only going about 30 miles per hour since she had just pulled out moments earlier. The impact was crazy! The back of her car was flattened upward, approximately seven feet in the air. The gas tank was full and pushed up against her seat. There was no back seat left at all. The spoiler on the trunk hit her in the back of the head and her car crumpled into her like an accordion. The impact pushed her into the steering wheel, which bent inward with the force of her body. The car was thrown like a rock in a slingshot, spinning around three times before somehow stopping just inches from oncoming traffic on a major freeway.

In no condition to drive, I called my dear friend who lived close by. She didn't understand me at first. We laughed later because she thought I said, "A tornado hit my house and sucked up Reeses!" I have no clue how she heard that, but finally the ambulance driver got on the phone and told her what had happened and she came immediately.

After seeing the wreckage, anyone's first thought would have been: that person didn't survive.

His Love Is Enough

We went to the hospital and, can you believe it, Lindsey didn't even need any stitches. It was a miracle! Lindsey had seven broken ribs, a bruised lung, scratches from thrown glass, and, thankfully, seat belt burns across her chest and pelvic area. The most critical concern was the swelling of her brain and short-term memory loss. She didn't remember anything past lunch the day of the accident and still doesn't to this day. Lindsey was in the intensive care unit for six days and was in pretty bad shape for three weeks. But Lindsey is OK! Praise the Lord! We believe Lindsey was saved on purpose for a purpose! We are thankful and we believe God heard and answered my specific prayers.

Lindsey was in an accident, but I didn't get the dreaded phone call. Instead, the Holy Spirit prompted me to go and hear the news face-to-face from an ambulance driver. I didn't have to wait hours to find out if she was OK. I knew she was conscious and moving and that's all I needed to know at the time! Lindsey lived and God got all the glory.

You may be asking, "Why did God answer your prayer but not the prayers of other mothers who may have prayed the same prayer?" I can't answer that. What I can share with you is this: when our relationship with the Lord is close, we trust in His faithfulness, no matter what the circumstance. His love is enough, whatever the outcome. It's unexplainable!

I have a friend who did get the dreaded phone call. And sadly, her daughter did pass away. Though the loss is intense, my friend is comforted by the fact many students and adults surrendered their lives to Jesus Christ at her daughter's funeral. God got the glory.

Another dear friend of mine, Gayla, was a precious, godly wife and mother. She loved Jesus, and everyone she met quickly became her friend. Those close to Gayla also knew that she had a fear of flying. One day, while at a special event, Gayla and the other attendees all had a surprise. A helicopter was going to take everyone to a restaurant where they would be dining that evening. Gayla and her husband were the first to take the ride. Although nervous, Gayla got on. Only moments later, Gayla's life was taken. In a split second the helicopter crashed.

Her husband survived, but Gayla was killed instantly. Do we grieve and question why God would take this young wife and mother of two? Yes, we do! We also know that God our Father loves us and knows our grief. And, He knows our future! The Lord had a plan and a purpose for Gayla; He has a plan for her children, for her husband, and ultimately He got the glory from this tragic accident. She lived to honor Him and now her family continues to live for Him even in the midst of their loss. This is our purpose: to live for and glorify God. Gayla did that! God's ways are not ours. We can't understand, but we can trust Him and His Word. Many of Gayla's friends and family who did not have a relationship with Jesus do now. They too have the promise of eternal life now and forever, just as Gayla did. Knowing heaven is our eternal home gives us hope and joy in the midst of our suffering. God is God. He is the Author and Finisher. The First and the Last. The Great I Am.

We cannot conceive all that God will do in this life. We cannot understand His ways, but we can trust His promise to be with us always. It's often in times of suffering and pain that we experience His great love for us, more than at any other time. It's in times of suffering that we draw closer to God. Can you see how times of suffering deepen our love for the Lord? Can you see how difficult times strengthen our character, develop perseverance, and deepen our trust in God?

Read the passage from the Book of Romans below.

We also rejoice in our sufferings, because we know that suffering produces perseverance; perseverance, character; and character, hope. And hope does not disappoint us, because God has poured out his love into our hearts by the Holy Spirit, whom he has given us.
—Romans 5:3–5 (NIV)

No matter the circumstance, I know when we love God with all our heart, all our mind, and all our soul, then we are truly free to love and be loved. And that's the life I want!

My Journal

The power of influence is amazing! Write your thoughts about something in this session that has influenced you.

~~~~~~

~~~~~~

~~~~~~

~~~~~~

Who are some people who have influenced your life? Who are some people that can you influence for God?

~~~~~~

~~~~~~

~~~~~~

Let me remind you of David in 1 Samuel 16. Some might have said, "He's just a shepherd in the fields tending a few sheep. What can he do?" But God said "I choose David to be king!" David was handpicked for a very significant purpose. I believe God has handpicked you for something, what would you imagine it to be?

~~~~~~

~~~~~~

~~~~~~

~~~~~~

If you're thinking you've already messed up too many times or your life situation is just too difficult to rise above, there's hope. Little sister, get those heavy negative thoughts out of your mind! Take a deep breath and tell yourself the truth: "God loves me so much! I am cherished by God! He has good plans for me!"

Cherished

I Am Cherished!

God's love is over the top! There are some experiences in life that are simply breathtaking. The experience never fades away. You can recall it like a snapshot. It will always be a cherished memory. No one can take away the experience, because it was yours. Oh, do I have an over-the-top kind of story to share with you!

Years ago I had the privilege to go on a missions trip to Romania with several others from my church. There were six adults and seven students. Talk about snapshots—there are many! It would be great if you could see the pictures on the screen of my mind, but since you can't, I will do my best to describe what I saw as I share my story.

This was my first trip outside the United States, and there was so much to consider: passports, culture, clothing, language, etc. However, it didn't take long to see that people are much the same no matter where you go. In fact, I instantly loved the people in Târgu Mure, Romania. Our mutual love for God created a bond that, well, is hard to express. I'm sure you too have met people for the first time and had an immediate sense of connection. Meeting these precious people was such a blessing, and I look forward to seeing them in heaven, if not before.

Our mission was to lead a summer camp for orphans and children who live on the street and under the train tracks in the city. At the camp, we provided a place for them to come for food and fun and to be surrounded by the love of God. We sang about Jesus, taught Bible stories, played games, went hiking, and tried to learn words in their language. We laughed a lot. It was great!

But there is one snapshot I want to tell you about in detail. Every morning, after breakfast, we had quiet time—a time to get alone with God. On this particular morning I walked over to a stream that was nearby the camp house. Picture the scene: a valley surrounded by lush mountains carpeted with vivid green grass. The pine trees had to be at least 60 feet tall and shaded every piece of land. Bright red strawberries peeked through the green ferns that grew down the sides of the mountains. It was a cool 62 degrees, and the sun rose just over the top of the mountain in front of me. I listened to the soft murmur of the water running over the rocks in the shallow stream. As I made my way over to a rock in the middle of the stream, my heart was full of praise to God, the Creator of it all.

After a few moments of enjoying the stillness of the moment, I opened my Bible and began to read John 10:1–21. Stop now and read this beautiful passage for yourself. Did you read it? If you didn't, please read it before going on. It will make my story so much better!

As I was reading, I heard something. *Bells? Where are they coming from?* Seconds later, out of the corner of my eye, I saw what I thought was a dog coming down the side of the mountain. *Wait! It's not a dog, it's a lamb.* Then another, and another, and another. There were many now, coming down the mountain and headed toward the field in front of me. Next I heard a voice. "Dah, dah!" and words I did not understand, but somehow I knew what he was saying by watching what he was doing. He was a shepherd leading his flock to water.

I was stunned, but at the same time my insides were leaping with joy. It was as though I was seeing a moving version of what I had just been reading. *Could this really be?* I wondered. Thankfully I have witnesses or who would believe it really happened?

I watched in amazement at what happened next. The shepherd had his little son with him, who helped herd the sheep into the gate of a fenced-in area. The shepherd held his staff and with every sheep that entered the gate, he hit his staff against the ground. It was obvious that he was counting his sheep. He motioned for the son to come over and

Cherished

stand by the gate. Then the shepherd proceeded to go back up into the mountain. After what seemed like only a moment, the shepherd came back down carrying a lamb around his neck.

Stop and read Matthew 18:12–14 and also Luke 15:3–7.

Are you crying yet? Oh my goodness! This is one of my all-time favorite Jesus stories! On this day God showed me how much He loves me! He gave me a priceless gift. He orchestrated every detail. Where I would be, the verses I would be reading, the shepherd and the sheep coming down the mountain into that field. All at just the right moment, a divine moment! I think God felt like showing off that day! He's wonderful! He's amazing! He's awesome! And He loves me!

God loves you too! He loves you even when you aren't doing everything right. Thank goodness, because none of us ever do *everything* right *all* the time. However, when you spend your life loving Him, desiring to do His will, I believe you too will experience some God-sized gifts!

What a Celebration!

I wish we could be together right now to worship the Father, to sing praises to Him. It has been wonderful to write of His amazing love, to read and study His love letters. I can think of nothing better than ending this study with a big celebration party in His honor.

What do you think? Can you see it? A huge banquet room decorated in white, silver, and crystal. Every chair covered in white with a silver bow tied on its back. Tables covered in white linens with iridescent organza overlays. Gorgeous, tall, centerpieces filled with white peonies, each looking a bit different in their elegant display. Mmmm, their sweet fragrance would fill the room! We could have stringed instruments playing beautiful music. There would be greetings, hugs, and laughter…so much joy! The guest list would include girls from every culture, from the smallest people groups and the largest cities. What would I wear? Something exquisite, that's for sure, and perhaps I could even splurge on some one-of-a-kind glass slippers. After, all, I am the daughter of the guest of honor, the King.

He orchestrated every detail. Where I would be, the verses I would be reading, the shepherd and the sheep coming down the mountain into that field. All at just the right moment, a divine moment! I think God felt like showing off that day!

It doesn't matter how old we are, it's so much fun to imagine, to dream. Seriously, how fun would that party be? I guess we'll have to wait for the party of all parties—the banquet that will be given in heaven one day. But until then, let us love one another, embrace each other with a hug or a kiss. Let's pray for each other when we think of one another. Let's make new friends and meet our neighbors. Smile at strangers who pass by and gladly hold the door open for those who are older than us. Let's genuinely love others and serve those who are in need. And let's applaud and welcome those to the family of God who accept His invitation and believe.

This sounds like a dream, like it can't really happen, but it can! God's love will make a difference! Lives will change. People will turn from their selfish and sinful ways and finally experience the freedom that is only found in Jesus Christ!

Everything we have studied on this journey together has been about love. Since God is love, everything has been about Him! And now you know where to find that love here on Earth. God's love is found in His children. In you! In me!

Everything we have studied on this journey together has been about love. Since God is love, everything has been about Him!

Cherished

Sadly, we throw the word *love* around so much that it often loses its truest meaning. So, I'd like to talk about a different word for a minute. *Cherished* is a word that describes a love that shows intentional devotion.

"What exactly does that mean?" you ask. *Intentional* describes an act done on purpose, premeditated, planned. And *devotion* indicates loyalty, dedication, commitment; it shows a fondness. I'm sure you agree that you don't use those words to describe pizza or shoes or your favorite outfit. Just think about it for a moment.

What is something that you can sincerely say you cherish?

I keep them in a box. Notes, written on little pieces of paper, that have no value to anyone but me. Why do I keep them? Because my daddy wrote them and his memory is so dear to me. He passed away years ago, but

Cherished

these little pieces of paper are notes he wrote to me during the last months of his life. I will always cherish them! Seeing his handwriting, reading his words, there's just something about it. I can hear his voice. I remember his smile; the way he sang hymns on Sunday morning at church; the way he loved nature; his hugs; the way he loved me and my mom and my family; how his life was a reflection of Jesus in his love and service for others! I could go on and on but really it all comes down to the way he *cherished* me.

In my kitchen are two small frames. One frame holds a picture of Bruce and me at his surprise 40th birthday party. I love to look at it! I cherish the memory of us together, happy, healthy, friendships, the celebration of his life; I cherish Bruce, I cherish our marriage. The other frame shows the faces of Lindsey and Holly at just four and two years old. It's a two-by-two-inch square frame that sits next to the other one. When I miss my girls I can look at that picture, and it takes me back. I hear giggles and soft little voices saying, "Hold me, Mommy, hold me." I cherish my girls. I've actually thought if there were ever a time I needed to grab a few things and leave my house immediately, I would grab these three things.

It might sound crazy to some because these pieces of paper and two tiny frames have no value. Oh yes they do! They do to me! The value is found in the memories that I cherish. Isn't the brain a magnificent creation? All I have to do is look at these items and it unlocks a treasure chest filled with the many blessings of my life.

"Do not store up for yourselves treasures on earth, where moth and rust destroy, and where thieves break in and steal. But store up for yourselves treasures in heaven where moth and rust do not destroy, and where thieves do not break in and steal. For where your treasure is, there your heart will be also."
—Matthew 6:19–21 (NIV)

God cherishes you so much that He wants you to live life on earth to the fullest. He knows that the key is to love Him and serve others. That's a life worth living. He knows this is what will bring you joy. But there's more! He adores you so much that He never wants to be apart from you so He made a way for you to be with Him forever. He cherishes you so much that the best is yet to come.

Anyone who does not love does not know God, for God is love. God showed how much he loved us by sending his one and only Son into the world so that we might have eternal life through him. This is real love not that we loved God, but that he loved us and sent his Son as a sacrifice to take away our sins. Dear friends, since God loved us that much, we surely ought to love each other. No one has ever seen God. But if we love each other, God lives in us, and his love has been brought to full expression in us.
—1 John 4:8–12

This, my little sister, is what it means to be cherished! No one else has ever done for us what God has done.

This, my little sister, is what it means to be cherished! No one else has ever done for us what God has done. He sent His only Son Jesus Christ to shed his blood on the Cross for you and for me and for anyone who believes. Therefore, it was intentional devotion, and He did this because He loves us that much.

God really does love you! You are cherished by God, the Creator of all things, the King of the world. He cherishes you!

"Faith, hope, and love. But the greatest of these is love" (1 Corinthians 13:13 NIV). The notes in the *Life Application Study Bible* (NLT) put it so well: "Love is the greatest of all human qualities, and it is an attribute of God himself. Faith is the foundation and content of God's message; hope is the attitude and focus; love is the action. When faith and hope are in line, you are free to love completely because you understand how God loves."

Please know that all I've written in this book is for God's glory, to show you that His love is extravagant! My hope is that after reading this study you will know God more deeply, through His Son, Jesus Christ. My hope is that you will long to love others and that you, my sweet sister, will understand your value and love the beautiful, unique person God has created you to be. Live life. Have fun. Expect great things. Love others. Follow God. My final wish for you is that you feel loved; even more, I pray that you know you are cherished by God...because you are!

Cherished

New Hope® Publishers is a division of WMU®, an international organization that challenges Christian believers to understand and be radically involved in God's mission. For more information about WMU, go to www.wmu.com. More information about New Hope books may be found at www.newhopepublishers.com. New Hope books may be purchased at your local bookstore.

If you've been blessed by this book, we would like to hear your story. The publisher and author welcome your comments and suggestions at: newhopereader@wmu.org

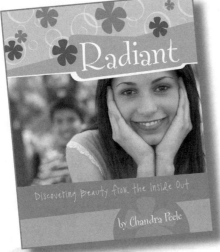
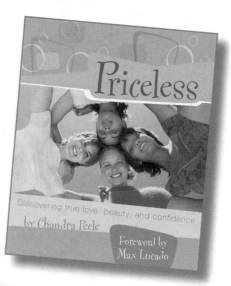
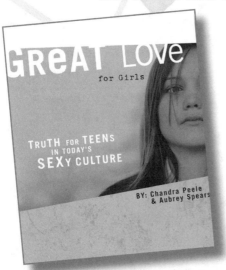